"WITH THE HELP OF

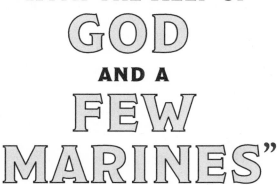

GOD

AND A

FEW

MARINES"

The Battles of Chateau Thierry and Belleau Wood

ALBERTUS W. CATLIN

WESTHOLME
Yardley

Westholme Publishing, LLC
904 Edgewood Road
Yardley, Pennsylvania 19067
Visit our Web site at www.westholmepublishing.com

First Printing September 2013
ISBN: 978-1-59416-188-9
Also available as an eBook.

Printed in the United States of America.

CONTENTS

INTRODUCTION

WHEN the Crown Prince of Germany started his drive down across the Chemin des Dames in the latter days of May, 1918, and penetrated as far as the Marne at Château-Thierry, Paris itself, only thirty-five miles away, was threatened as it had not been since Von Kluck was checked by Joffre in the first Battle of the Marne. The Allies had weakened their lines in this sector to stop the earlier drive in the Somme country to the northwest and the Germans took the weary French completely by surprise. With a tremendous weight of men, machine guns, and gas shells, they hacked their way through in a blunt, irresistible wedge, till the French, outnumbered, spent, demoralized, and with their resisting power diminished to the vanishing point, were forced to give way before the terrific onrush of force.

At the point nearest Paris the danger was acute. It seemed as though nothing human could prevent the German from attaining his objective. A cry for help arose. An American division was rushed to the front and thrown into the fray. Half of this division was composed of Marines, who were given the post of honour and danger at the centre. Most of them, though serving under seasoned officers, had seen but little of the action of battle. Could they stem the tide that threatened to engulf the capital of France? They were virtually untried, and they were called upon to whip the flower of the Kaiser's army, flushed with victory and enjoying all the advantage of momentum.

When the history of the Great War is written, it will be no easy task to assign to each of the titanic battles its proper place in the scale of importance, but if justice is done, the Battle of Belleau Wood will take its place beside that of Thermopylæ and the other crucial battles of world history. Here a mere handful of determined, devoted men, as numbers are reckoned to-day, turned the awful tide, and they were soldiers and Marines of the United States of America.

We shall need the perspective of time to judge of these things aright, but in the light of the present it is not too much to say that this mêlée in the woods, this bitter struggle for a bit of ground smaller than Central Park, marked the turning point of this whole war. For if the Marines had not driven the Germans out of Belleau Wood it must have gone hard with the Allies in that sector. The Germans would, in all probability, have been enabled in another day or two to bring up their reserves and their heavier guns, and nothing but a miracle could have saved Paris. It was the American who held that Metz-to-Paris road, and no less a personage than

Premier Clemenceau is authority for the statement that the United States Marines were unquestionably the saviours of the city. When the engagement was over and the Germans had been driven back, General Degoutte, commanding the Sixth Army of France, signed a special order changing the name of the Bois de Belleau to the Bois de la Brigade de Marine.

The Marines were called upon to do the impossible, and because there is no such word in their code, they did it. They left in that wood some of the best blood of America, but, outnumbered and inexperienced as they were, they fought that last-stand fight to a finish and they stopped the Hun.

There is a reason for all this, and the people back home ought to know something about it. Time was when the Marine was looked upon as a mere handy man for the Navy, a sort of web-footed policeman who was neither soldier nor sailor. That time has long since passed, but even to-day the average American has but a vague idea of what a Marine is.

Something has made the U. S. Marine a name to conjure with in the four quarters of the globe, has won for him the soubriquet of *Teufelhund* from the Boche himself. Personnel, training, tradition, and experience have all had a part in it, and that imponderable but all-powerful quality which we call *esprit de corps*. The Marine is a trained athlete, a picked man, a he creature with muscles and a jaw, whose motto is "kill or be killed," and who believes with all his soul that no man on earth can lick him. And it comes pretty near to being so. He is own

brother to the British Marine, of whom Kipling
wrote:

"An' after I met 'im all over the world, a-doin' all kinds
of things,
Like landin' 'isself with a Gatlin' gun to talk to them
'eathen kings;
'E sleeps in an 'ammick instead of a cot, an' 'e drills with
the deck on a slew,
An' 'e sweats like a Jolly—'Er Majesty's Jolly—soldier
an' sailor too!
For there isn't a job on the top o' the earth the beggar
don't know, nor do—
You can leave 'im at night on a bald man's 'ead, to paddle
'is own canoe—
'E's a sort of a bloomin' cosmopolouse—soldier an' sailor
too."

General Catlin has told a graphic, eye-witness
story of the Battle of Belleau Wood, but he has
done much more than this. He has given us an in-
sight into the making of a Marine, and the American who can read the whole story of it without a
soul-searching thrill of patriotic pride is no American
at all.

Of General Catlin himself, who, as Colonel of the
Sixth Regiment of Marines, commanded the forces
at Belleau Wood, I feel that something should be
said, though it would be the worst of taste to tack
a fulsome eulogy to the narrative of a man so thoroughly straightforward and modest as he. His men
idolize him, and perhaps that tells the whole story.

Brigadier General Albertus Wright Catlin is a

Marine of the Marines. Born in Gowanda, N. Y.,
December 1, 1868, he was appointed to the Naval
Academy from Minnesota in May, 1886. He graduated from Annapolis with the Class of 1890. His
two-years' cruise as midshipman followed. The
Marines seemed to offer the best chance for active
service at that time and upon his return from the
cruise he applied for a commission in the Corps.
On July 1, 1892, he was made a Second Lieutenant
of Marines.

He was commissioned First Lieutenant in April,
1893, and served with that rank during the Spanish
War, being the officer of Marines on the battleship
Maine when she was sunk in Havana Harbour.

He was commissioned Captain in 1899 and Major
in 1905. Active service followed, including the
occupation of Vera Cruz in 1914, when he was in
command of the Marines that were landed from the
fleet. In 1915 he became Lieutenant Colonel. During 1916 he studied at Fort Leavenworth and at the
National War College, receiving his Colonel's commission in the same year. He graduated from the
War College in May, 1917.

At the outbreak of the Great War he was placed
in charge of the Marine training camp at Quantico,
Va., and went to France as Colonel of the newly
formed Sixth Regiment of Marines. He led the
Marines in the attack on Belleau Wood on June 6,
1918, and there he received the bullet wound through
the right lung that placed him temporarily on the
sick list. As a result of his masterly leadership in

that stirring and critical engagement he was commissioned Brigadier General in July and was decorated with the French Legion of Honour and the Croix de Guerre.

General Catlin himself has something to say about American football and its relation to the American fighting spirit. I will only add that he captained his team at Annapolis and played left halfback there for three years. Later he played on the Navy team during his two-years' midshipman cruise and again with the Columbia Athletic Club in Washington. I think I can see him ploughing through the Army line in those days as vividly as I see him leading the boys at Belleau Wood. It may be that we should revise the Duke of Wellington's statement that Waterloo was won on the cricket fields of Eton and Harrow; one is tempted to suggest that Paris was saved on the gridiron at Franklin Field.

It was my privilege to spend some days with him in Hot Springs, Va., where he was recuperating. He is a young man of fifty, powerful of build, and of medium height, with iron-grey hair, an eye as clear and frank as a child's, and a face about as weak and effeminate as Plymouth Rock. It is largely jaw. His is the genial nature of a man who fights when he has to fight and at no other time. Directness is an outstanding quality of his, and I was much impressed by the remarkable accuracy of his memory and his grasp of military situations.

He was wearing without ostentation the silver star of his rank on his shoulder and the wound and service chevrons on his sleeves. On his breast were the coloured ribbon bands, two of them, indicating the actions in which he has taken part in various wars and minor expeditions. He wore the khaki service uniform, and in his blouse, perilously near the heart, were two neatly mended holes, one in front and one in back, where the German sniper's bullet had drilled him. "A sort of souvenir," said he, smiling.

One day he showed me quite casually a cablegram announcing that he had been awarded the French Croix de Guerre and the decoration of the Legion of Honour. I believe he was the first American general officer to receive these honours for heroism in action. Later I obtained a copy of his citation, which was translated as follows:

Colonel A. W. Catlin: Field Officer who, on June 6, 1918, was placed in charge of a delicate operation, particularly difficult of execution, and made an undoubted success of it; combines the finest military qualities with a noble spirit of devotion and self-sacrifice; when severely wounded by a bullet during the action, asked the officer with him, as he fell, if he had really been wounded facing the enemy and if his men were continuing to progress.

The following is a copy of General Bundy's letter recommending Colonel Catlin's promotion:

As former commander of the Second Division, of which the Marine Brigade forms a part, I recommend Colonel Catlin, Sixth Regiment Marines, for promotion to the grade of Brigadier General in the Marine Corps. Colonel

Catlin has commanded his regiment with unceasing industry and great ability in all phases of open and trench warfare. He was wounded while gallantly leading a part of it against the enemy north of Château-Thierry. He is entitled to promotion in recognition of his splendid service on the field of battle.

It is not necessary to dilate upon what these things mean, nor how they affected me. As for General Catlin, I believe he is prouder of the bronze insignia of the Marines than of all the others together.

He saw the things he writes about; of them he was no inconsiderable part. He led the boys at Belleau Wood, and no one man did more than he to save Paris. That, I think, is what makes his story a historical document of the first importance as well as a narrative of thrilling interest. For the rest, I need only to call attention to his pride in his men and his organization, and the stalwart patriotism of the soldier that runs through it all.

"With the help of God and a few Marines" is a phrase that has been attributed to nearly every naval hero from John Paul Jones to Admiral Dewey, and it fits. It describes a hundred instances in which the honour of the United States has been upheld beyond the seas; it somehow expresses the very spirit of the Corps; and it tells in a nutshell the story of the fight in Belleau Wood and the saving of Paris from the Hun.

W. A. D.

PART I

MARINES TO THE FRONT!

"WITH THE HELP OF GOD AND A FEW MARINES"

CHAPTER 1

What Is a Marine?

SINCE it appears that I am fated for an interval to lay aside the sword and take up the less congenial pen, I should prefer to begin at once with the thing that is uppermost in my mind—the story of the United States Marines in France. So fresh in my memory are those days in the trenches and the dark, moonless nights, pregnant with we knew not what possibilities, when the boys stole over the top on their first patrol duties. How eagerly, how anxiously we watched them, as a mother watches the first steps of her child, to discover whether they would face the music and do the job as a Marine should. We knew they would, but still we watched, and when they came back with what they went for, we breathed deep and faced the next task with confidence.

It was in those days that good American blood was spilt out there in No Man's Land, in the midst of the barbed wire and the lurking menace. We looked upon our dead, and had the Hun known, he might well have trembled then.

I recall so vividly those busy days in camp, and the spirit that seemed to be loosed when the great call came; the long, forced ride on camions through the little, smiling villages, where the good French people lined the streets, waving American flags and throwing flowers at us; the tense, electrical feeling in the air when at last we knew that we were face to face with the victorious Prussian, and the awful, earnest, exultant moment when we went in to fight. And, waking or sleeping, I can still see before me the dark threat of Belleau Wood, as full of menace as a tiger's foot, dangerous as a live wire, poisonous with gas, bristling with machine guns, alive with snipers, scornfully beckoning us to come on and be slain, waiting for us like a dragon in its den. Our brains told us to fear it, but our wills heard but one command, to clean it out, and I can still see before my very eyes those waves in the poppy-spattered wheat-field as the steady lines of our Marines went in.

Those are the things that surge to the tip of my pen, but I have first, I feel, another duty to perform. I must tell something of the men who did this glorious thing and of the spirit that drove them on.

A fight is a fight, and few red-blooded men can resist the thrill of it, but it is not my purpose to glorify a fight nor to sing the Song of Hate. The Marine fights because fighting is the immediate and essential means to an end. He trusts implicitly the judgment of his superiors that the end justifies the means, not with the blind trust of the docile German, but from a well grounded and well understood principle. For a hundred years and more the Marines have been called upon when there was a critical need for action, and they have learned to take the need for granted and to act forthwith. They have never been deceived and they never hesitate. That is part of their creed.

It is because they have a creed that this narrative is written. Perhaps it is a creed that all men might follow with profit; we like to think so. The American Marine fights as well as any man on earth, and his fighting is worth writing about if any fighting is, but it is the thing back of his fighting that counts. There are significant, fundamental things that mean more in the philosophy of human and national life than even the taking of a stronghold and the blocking of an advance.

Who are these Marines? A bare thousand of them challenged death in Belleau Wood with the same spirit that drove on the Six Hundred at Balaklava. What sort of man did this thing? Where did he come from? What made him fit to go in with the first and bear the brunt while the rest of America was getting ready to make war on Germany?

In the first place, the Marines were ready, as no other group of American fighting men, with the exception of the Engineers, was ready. I think I can say this truthfully and without disparagement to any other branch of the service. Our problems were perhaps not so serious as those of the Army.

I know something of their difficulties, for we were billeted close to the Ninth and 23rd Infantry in France during the spring of 1918. The Marines, though the Corps had been greatly expanded, had smaller numbers to handle, and we believe that our system of training was more highly perfected. Also, we had a certain advantage in personnel, both in men and new officers, as I shall show later on.

At the outbreak of the war the Army organization underwent radical changes. Not only were new regiments formed, but the numbers were changed from 1,000 to 3,600 men to a regiment. The old regiments were broken up so that the seasoned soldiers might serve as nuclei for the new ones, and they had to be spread out so thin that there were only about 300 of them to a regiment, or some 8 per cent. Moreover, it was thought best to hold the National Guard regiments together, so that the regular Army had to depend for its enlargement upon volunteer enlistments and a forced recruiting campaign. When this did not suffice, the Army was compelled to fill its ranks with volunteers —not picked men—from the draft. This created a tremendous problem in the matter of training, the majority of the regular Army being nothing more than raw recruits, and it is no discredit to them that they did not turn at once into efficient troops.

As will be seen later, the larger part of our expeditionary force of Marines was also composed of new men, but their training began at once under more favourable auspices. At Quantico, and later in France, they were drilled without let-up by experienced officers of the Marines. Then came participation in trench warfare, and one year after the United States had declared war, every one of those rookies had been converted into a died-in-the-wool Marine, while the Army was still making soldiers.

I make these statements in no spirit of criticism or invidious comparison, but simply to show, if I can, why the Marines were the ones chosen to go in first. Whatever the reason, they were ready first. It is part of the history of which they are so proud that they have nearly always been sent in first, because it is a fundamental part of their creed to be always ready. Their mottoes are "First to Fight" and "Semper Fidelis."

These are days of enormous armies and organization on a tremendous scale, but small numbers do unquestionably make possible a closer human relationship, and that, in our experience, means increased confidence, a more effective discipline, and *esprit de corps*. The Marines have always been, comparatively speaking, an organization of small numbers; those who have read of their world-wide achievements in the past perhaps do not realize how small. Previous to the Spanish War the entire Corps was but half the size of a modern regiment, and the forces which so often brought order out of chaos in turbulent lands and put to rout armies of rapacious revolutionaries were few in numbers though mighty, like a squad of New York policemen quelling a riot. Americans have come to take it as a matter of course that a Marine should be able to do the work of ten ordinary men, and the Marines have come to that belief, too.

Numbering only 1,800 at the outbreak of the Spanish War, the Marine Corps was steadily enlarged until, in 1918, there were nearly 60,000 Marines in the service or in training. Though still a small unit, as modern military figures go, it will be seen that the Corps has been obliged to absorb a large percentage of increase, most of it since the United States joined in the Great War, and it may be well to note that, as it stands to-day, the Corps is more than twice the size of the United States Army at the outbreak of the Spanish War. And this increase has been accomplished without any depreciation in personnel. The Marines, all through their forced war-time recruiting, have maintained their high standards and have consistently rejected all applicants who were not of the first calibre.

With these comparatively small numbers, and with this effort to maintain the highest standard in personnel, the Marines have directed every effort toward securing mobility, which, with us, is a synonym for readiness. The things we have to do usually have to be done quickly if at all, and our arrangements are such that when the call comes we have nothing whatever to do but go ahead. Until we had to make special preparations for the war work in France, we had no regimental or company organizations. Every man was a member of the

Marine Corps and of nothing else, and he was prepared to serve under any of the officers. There was never any delay due to the filling up of a company quota. When a job needed to be done the available officers were chosen and the available men assembled, and off they went as a complete unit. If there was trouble abroad, a naval vessel was sent, and on its decks were always the Marines, ready to land and serve as engineers, electricians, artillery, infantry, or even cavalry, or as Uncle Sam's policemen. If a call came that required the reserves, officers were summoned by wire to Philadelphia and the required number of men from Norfolk, Portsmouth, Boston, New York, Washington, or wherever they might chance to be. Their kits were always ready and they arrived as quickly as the trains could bring them. Meanwhile, the quartermaster's department in Philadelphia, fully equipped for all emergencies, was rushing the necessary supplies aboard ship, and by the time the men had assembled—in twenty-four hours perhaps—the whole expedition was ready to start for the ends of the earth and it was simply up to the captain of the ship.

This sort of mobility and preparedness is an essential part of the very spirit and tradition of the Corps, bred into the Marine from the start and understood by him as merely a part of the day's work. It rather distinguishes this branch of the service from all others. In no others has it been required to quite the same degree. And does it not explain, in part at least, why the Marines were ready with the first over there in France?

As to the individual soldier, there is more than one sort of preparedness, and we like to think that that of the Marine is the most effective kind. The German soldier had been prepared for years. He knew his number and his place in the ranks. He was taught what to do with the implements of war. But he was prepared for just one thing—the kind of onslaught that his overlords thought was all there would be to the war. He was prepared for the thing they had carefully figured out would happen; they considered it not worth their while to prepare the poor tool for anything else.

The United States Marine, on the other hand, is prepared, so far as it is humanly possible to prepare a man, for anything that may happen. He is ready for the unforeseen emergency.

Discipline is no less a fundamental plank in the Marine platform than is preparedness. There is a sense in which the Marines are not the best disciplined soldiers in the world. As mechanical, insentient automatons, moving with clock-like precision, they must hand the palm to the Boches. The discipline of the Marines, however, is thorough, and we make no apology for it. Respect for officers and absolute, unquestioning obedience to orders is taught from the beginning, but we proceed on the principle that we are dealing with intelligent men. We believe in leaving something to their own initiative and resourcefulness, and the theory has panned out on a hundred occasions. When we ordered the Marines to go into Belleau Wood, there was no question of obedience. No German could have responded more steadily or promptly. But we did not send them in blindfolded. Every man was told by his officers just what we were up against and what was expected of him as an individual, and they fought the better for it. As it turned out, that fight called for nothing so much as star individual play, and no machine that can work only when in perfect gear could have done what those Marines did in the Bois de Belleau.

That is what I mean when I speak of discipline. It is the discipline of the trained football team, which would go to pieces if the signals were not followed, but which would do but sluggish work if each man were not on his toes to snatch up the fumbled ball and dash around the end without interference.

I don't know that there is much to be said about the discipline of the Marines in a technical sense. It differs but little from the discipline of the Army and Navy. The regulations are practically the same. Yet there is one point of difference which perhaps explains our success with the men. With our smaller detachments, the officers come into closer touch with the men, and a better mutual understanding makes for a more effective discipline. Furthermore, the system by which the working detachments are organized, with no previously established companies or platoons, brings each of the officers from time to time in close contact with a larger number of the men than is possible under the Army system. Whatever the cause, I know that on more than one occasion both Army and Navy officers have of their own accord pointed to the Marines as models for their own men in the matter of discipline.

There is a special training which the Marine recruits must undergo that explains much regarding the quality and effectiveness of the finished product. Of the details of that training I will speak more at length in another place. They are taught to shoot straight and to obey commands with a snap and vigour that few other military organizations ever attain. To this system of training we owe much, for when the Marines went in at Belleau Wood, but a short year after most of them had enlisted, they were acknowledged to be one of the sharpest shooting, hardest fighting brigades in France.

There is among the Marines, to a noteworthy degree, readiness and mobility, there is intensive training, and there is discipline. There is also the tradition and history of the Corps of which every Marine is proud. It means something to us, that history. We have a reputation to live up to, and we do not mean to lower our record or bring disgrace to our insignia. I shall speak in some detail of that history later on. It is an honourable one, and about it has grown up a tradition that amounts to a sort of faith. In so many fights, big and little, the Marines have come through with flying colours, with the job cleanly done, that they never expect to do otherwise. The Marine has learned to believe in his organization and in himself. He acknowledges no man his superior in a fight, and meeting odds is but the thing he is trained for.

Since the United States of America became a world power, the United States Marine has been Uncle Sam's advance scout. He has been called "the can-opener of the Army." He comes as near to being an international policeman as any man on earth.

The *Washington Times* in an editorial once gave a fairly accurate description of the Corps. "Kipling," it said, "is the only man who could sing the song of the American Marines quite worthily. They are the men who have done about all the fighting under the American flag since the Civil War, save in the little conflict with Spain. Under all skies and climates, they are always at the point where they are needed; the skirmish line, the police patrol of our Government, the guardians of National dignity and American citizens wherever there may be threat of trouble. The young American with an ambition for real adventure, with wish to see and learn the art of war, has in recent years been commended to the Marines. If there is trouble, it means Marines to the front, first to get orders, first in motion, first ashore, first to fire. There is no finer body of fighting men in all the world, none more thoroughly seasoned or widely experienced."

A Colonel of the British Army, a real student of military affairs, once made this assertion: "The best equipped body of its size in the world is the United States Marine Corps; the second best is the Canadian Northwest Mounted Police, and the third best the Pennsylvania State Constabulary." And Admiral Dewey said, "No finer military organization exists in the world."

Esprit de corps—that is the thing that has come out of all this training and tradition. It is a difficult thing to weigh, to describe, to analyze, for it belongs in the realm of the spiritual. We only know that it exists, that it is woven into the very warp and woof of our Corps, that it is an invaluable quality for the fighting man.

They tell the story of some distinguished visitors who were passing along the cots in a military hospital in France. On one of these cots lay a man, quite still, with his face buried in the pillow. Something about him caused one of the visitors to remark, "I think this must be an American soldier." From the depths of the pillow came a muffled voice —"Hell, no; I'm a Marine!"

CHAPTER II

To France!

WHEN the United States declared war on Germany, a thrill went through the Marine Corps, for we were fighting men all and we learned that Marines were to be rushed over to France to take their stand on the Frontier of Liberty beside the battle-scarred veterans of France and Great Britain. War-time recruiting began at once and hundreds of promising applicants thronged our doors. We weeded them out—sifted them down unmercifully, and the best of them we packed off to Paris Island, S. C., and Mare Island, Cal., to be made into Marines. An overseas training camp was established at Quantico, Va., and I went down to take charge. There we received the graduates from the regular training stations as fast as they could be turned out, and through the summer and fall of 1917 we drilled 'em and we drilled 'em, until they were fit to go up against any foe on earth. We taught them to shoot straight and to use the bayonet, we had them mopping up trenches and cutting wire, we hardened them with hikes and we got them to handle machine guns like baby carriages. We filled them full to bursting with the spirit of the Corps and then we shipped them across to France to fight. And did they fight? You shall see.

The Marine is traditionally proud, and I cannot truthfully say that we take any drastic measures to suppress that pride. He is proud of his record of being ready first and first on the job. But he knows his equal when he sees him, and the Marine is never backward with a word of praise for the fellow who is able to leap into the breach before him and get into the fighting first.

The first Americans to draw the blood of the Beast were the Engineers, and to them we accord our meed of honour. We know what they are like, for we, too, have to turn our hands quickly to the task that comes uppermost and do it with the will and the skill of men. The world now knows what that little force of Engineers did, how they got to the front before the Kaiser and his followers fully realized that the great western republic had come into the war against them, how the sight of those sturdy Yankees brought hope to overwrought France, how they buckled down to their appointed task, one of the most difficult in the whole military régime, and how, when the need arose, they threw down their tools and picked up arms and proceeded to kill Germans. I hope some day a book will be written about the Engineers, as this one is being written about the Marines.

The Engineers were the first to land on French soil, but the Marines were a close second. After General Pershing and his staff had gone to Paris, the first regular fighting troops from this country to be landed in France consisted of four regiments of Army regulars and one of Marines.

Two months after war was declared the Marines were ready. In June, 1917, Colonel C. A. Doyen, in command of the Fifth Regiment of Marines, landed in France at St. Nazarre, near Brest, at the northern extremity of the Bay of Biscay. Of this first regiment to go to France, two battalions were from Philadelphia, and one was made up of our Quantico boys.

One battalion of the Fifth was left at St. Nazarre under Major Westcott for provost duty, remaining there for several months. Others were sent on provost duty to other parts of France; one company remained till the end of the war. But it is important service, nevertheless. Until January, 1918, the Marines did all the provost work for the American forces, for they were best equipped for just that sort of thing. They acted as military police in various places, policed the villages and cafés, had charge of American camps and debarkation ports, guarded the lines of communication and the various bases, and helped to keep in hand the flood of incoming troops.

Not all of the Fifth, however, was assigned to provost duty. Some of them went at once to a training area about 150 miles east of Paris, where they went into regular training with French troops as part of the First Division. Five full companies were able to complete this training.

In July we sent over a base battalion for the Fifth, 1,000 men under Lieutenant-Colonel Bearss. They went to Bordeaux for provost duty and until January, 1918, Bearss was Base Commander at Bordeaux.

In September the Sixth was ready. We sent over one battalion in September and I followed with the supply, Headquarters Company, and machine gun company in October. Doyen was made Brigadier General and took over the Fifth and Sixth as a brigade, Colonel Neville going over in December to take command of the Fifth.

I must tell something about this Sixth Regiment of mine. In the first place it must be borne in mind that it was an aggregation as new and untried as any regiment of the National Army, but what stuff we had in it! The officers, from captain up, and fifty or so of the non-commissioned officers were old-time Marines, but the junior officers and all of the privates were new men. But they were not like most rookies. They were of superior quality throughout, and they had been through the intensive training of the Marine Corps. By the time they were through with the training on French soil I doubt if any Army officer could have discovered the slightest trace of newness about them. They acted like veterans; they thought like veterans; and all because of that training and the material they were to start with.

If we had had time and opportunity to pick our men individually from the whole of the United

States I doubt whether we should have done much better. They were as fine a bunch of upstanding American athletes as you would care to meet, and they had brains as well as brawn. Sixty per cent of the entire regiment—mark this—sixty per cent of them were college men. Two-thirds of one entire company came straight from the University of Minnesota.

More than that, we had the pick of the men from the military colleges, because we were the first to pick. Of our young lieutenants a large number were college athletes. There was Lagore of Yale; Bastien of Minnesota, an All-America end; Moore and Murphy of Princeton; Maynard of the University of Washington; Overton, the Yale runner, who was killed in the offensive last summer, and a dozen others who won fame on the gridiron, track, and diamond while the United States was yet at peace. When you read of what these men did in Belleau Wood and Bouresches, remember who they were, and perhaps their exploits will seem less unbelievable.

The Turk will fight like a fiend; the Moro's trade is slaying; it was Fuzzy Wuzzy who broke a British square; the Boche will move in mass formation into the face of death like a ferry-boat entering its slip; but when the final show-down comes, when the last ounce of strength and nerve is called for, when mind and hand must act like lightning together, I will take my chances with an educated man, a free-born American with a trained mind. Unquestionably, the intelligent, educated man makes, in the long run, the best soldier. There is no place for the mere brute in modern warfare. It is a contest of brains as well as of brawn, and the best brains win. The American colleges doubtless supposed that they were turning men into scholars; when the test came they found they had been training soldiers.

We sent over one battalion of the Sixth in September; most of the others went across in October and November. The crossing was no easy matter, for the transport service was still inadequate, and the Marines had to depend upon the over-worked and over-crowded naval transportation. They disembarked at St. Nazarre and one battalion under Major John A. Hughes was left there to assist the Engineers and stevedores in the effort to bring order out of chaos in that swarming port. Another battalion was landed at Brest in November, under Major Sibley, and was sent on to Bordeaux, where they worked with the Engineers on the railroads, docks, etc. I arrived in October with my staff, a machine gun company, and the Headquarters Company, and proceeded to Bordeaux, where I had charge of the camps in that vicinity. The last battalion, under Major Holcomb, came in February, completing the Sixth Regiment of Marines.

How the boys took to the new life in France, and how things looked to them over there, may be gathered in part from the following letter from a Marine private to his father:

Somewhere in France.

DEAR FATHER:—

Write to Quantico and tell Nelson Springer to take salt water soap with him when he crosses. He will appreciate the advice. That is the one thing which bothered me on the trip across. I didn't worry about U-boats nor the fact that I had to sleep under a life-boat on the deck, completely dressed and burdened with a life belt and a canteen filled with fresh water. Nor has the fact annoyed me the least bit that I never took my clothes off after we started for France. But having to wash in salt water, and none too much at that, was the nearest approach to a hardship I experienced. There is nothing so sticky as the after effect of a salt-water face wash.

I am still yearning for a wash like the one I had on the train when we pulled out of Washington. The Red Cross girls fed us sandwiches and coffee. Those girls got up in the middle of the night to feed us, and they looked so clean and cheerful. I haven't seen anything half so clean since we left them, but we have managed to multiply their good cheer.

Of course, all of us didn't, for in spite of the excellent weather many of the men were seasick, and who could be cheerful then? There were a good many "abandon ship drills," but they were most humane about leaving us alone at night. The food was about what we got at Quantico, but we had to stand in line half the day to get a look in. After eating we would stand in another slowly moving line to wash the mess gear. I used bread to clean mine and found it served the purpose admirably. Lines of men wound all over the ship, a large part of them below decks. Only the fittest survived, and you may guess that I didn't miss a meal.

Old women and children dressed in black seem to be the chief inhabitants of Paris. I was surprised to hear the newsies crying "New York Herald," much the same as our news butchers do. In fact, Paris is quite American-ized. We bought nuts and apples from the natives as we marched out of the city, eating them on the hike.

I know where I am camping even if I cannot tell it, for we visited a few miles from here when we all came abroad. We are quarantined, for some unknown reason, in a field. The scenery is beautiful but it rains most of the time, which keeps us busy making drain ditches around our shelter-halves or "pup tents."

We are not allowed to give our washing to the French women whom we can see washing at the spring holes in the next field, nor can we make any purchases over the fence, so I'm saving a lot of money. Occasionally I try my French on the children who sit on the fence all day long and watch us. They think it very funny. They are great pals and make the most comical little playmates imaginable.

One of the most humorous features of our life here is that every one of the boys seems to think he is making history. Although we have had no chance to see action, if peace were declared to-morrow we would have enough to talk about the rest of our lives. It is strange how im-portant that phrase, "the rest of our lives," has become.

Dad, I want to tell you that I'm mighty glad I'm in France. Some of the things I've told you may sound like hardships, but they're not. It's all a part of the game. Every little detail in the life of the camp seems shadowed by some adventure—something new in store for us. The routine and the food are much the same as they were in America, but it all seems so different.

My tent mate has lifted the poncho on the open end of the tent. The inference is that he will soon come in and then all my time will be taken by seeing that he does not touch my side of the tent roof, for if he does it will start leaking. In some miraculous way we manage to keep the four-by-six-foot spot under the tent fairly dry. He is taking off his shoes so that the mud won't get on the blankets.

It is a matter of great speculation when we will be released from our restriction to camp, but we all hope to get our luck back soon.

Love to all,

DICK.

During the latter part of 1917 we had Marines doing provost duty all over France—at Havre, Tours, and a dozen other places, and even at Southampton, England. On January 1st the Marines were relieved of all provost duty by the 41st Division of Infantry—National Guardsmen. We were then assembled in a training area near Bourmont in the Verdun region, some fifty miles back of the lines. The Fifth was billeted in four little French towns and the Sixth in five. Here, for over two months, we engaged in the hardest kind of intensive training under French tutelage, a battalion of the 77th French Infantry being sent to us for that purpose.

Three English-speaking French officers were attached to each regiment in an advisory capacity, to instruct us in the elaborate system of trench orders and all the other details of trench fighting as developed in this war. They were splendid men and very helpful.

A series of trenches was dug near the town where the French troops were billeted, and part of our training included from four to six hours' work in these trenches several days each week. They were located eight miles from the nearest American town and thirteen from the farthest, so that our boys had to march sixteen to twenty-six miles a day, with a full pack, including intrenching tools, in addition to the hard work in the trenches. And this was not all. Our men were subject to hurry calls at any time of the night or day. There were forced marches to the trenches, occupation and relief at night, patrol work, sham raids, gas and raid signals, and all the rest of it. They were drilled constantly in trench organization, signal systems, and all the details of trench warfare as it existed at the front. And all this in addition to the routine drill of the Marines.

It was winter, cold and often stormy, but the weather made no difference. The training went forward every day, and manœuvres were executed in snowstorms. I can't say the boys liked it. Who would? But they learned their lessons with surprising aptitude and became as hard as nails.

And it was some satisfaction to learn that we had won official approval. While we were in the training area General Pershing came to inspect the brigade, and his comment was, "I only wish I had 500,000 of these Marines!"

I believe we had an easier time of it at that than the Army units that were billeted near us, for we were in rather better shape when we started in. All the more credit is due the Infantry, perhaps, because its units got into shape at all under such difficulties.

It was farming country where we were billeted, with little towns and villages scattered all over the map. In France the farmers do not live in isolated farmhouses as they do in this country. Their homes are in the villages and their farms outside. It would have been pretty country under some circumstances, and the towns picturesque, but this was the dreary winter season and the villages looked a bit forlorn. The pinch of war was everywhere in evidence. The inhabitants were chiefly old people and children, the younger men being with the Army and the younger women and girls having gone away to work in the munition plants. I fancy our boys brought a bit of colour and the joy of life into some of those desolate lives. I know they were sorry to see us go. At least, we left those villages cleaner and more comfortable than when we went into them, for we had religiously policed them and cleaned the streets.

One thing that struck me while in this training area was the remarkable efficiency of the French Forestry Department. Our food was furnished by the supply service of the American Army in France, but our fuel we had to cut for ourselves. This was arranged for by the French Government, and foresters and district officers were sent down to supervise the work. Not a tree was cut that the foresters had not marked, and not a twig was allowed to be wasted. There was none of that slap-dash, extravagant lumbering such as we Americans have so foolishly indulged in, but a careful, scientific selection of such timber as might be cut without robbing the forests. It was merely a matter of beneficial thinning out, and when this war is over, France will still have intact and flourishing such of her forests as the shells have spared. Necessity has taught her this; must we in America wait for the pinch of necessity?

In spite of exposure and not infrequent exhaustion, the health of our men was remarkably good during this training period. And I don't think they were unhappy. They were too busy for that. Nor did we have any trouble with drink or other forms of vice, partly because of the lack of opportunity and partly because of the strict regulations. And I do not think there will be much trouble of this sort in the American armies so long as General Pershing is at the helm. He is a man of inflexible determination, is Pershing, and he made up his mind at the outset that his soldiers should lose none of their effectiveness through drink or the results of vice. And he is succeeding as no other commander has ever succeeded in the history of the world. He has succeeded to such an extent that even the British have sent over a commission to find out how he accomplished it. And I am convinced that the average American soldier will return from the insidious perils of military life a cleaner and better man than when he went over. Americans can hardly overestimate the importance of this achievement. It is a thing for us, as a civilized nation, to be proud of and to thank God for.

During this tedious preliminary period of training the spirit of our Marines was, indeed, remarkable. It remained so all through the trench life that followed and through the bitter fighting that came after that. Cheerfulness is an outstanding quality of the American everywhere in France, and that has helped the Allied morale materially. As testimony, let me quote Private Horace W. Grey, of Tecumseh, Mich., who, some months later, lay in the Brooklyn Naval Hospital, cheerfully contemplating a stump where his left leg had been. Grey was hit by fragments of a high explosive shell that had first struck a rock, his company having just moved up into the battle line at Château-Thierry.

"I must speak of the high morale of the Marines," said he. "To me it is the most wonderful thing of all. There is never a gloomy moment. If some man should seem a little moody his companions make a special effort to kid him along until the sky grows brighter. No matter whether they were in box cars, the trenches, or battered Belleau Wood, they were always in buoyant spirits.

"You should have seen the little trumpeters. I remember time and again in the trenches when one of these youngsters would yell out shrilly as a shell came near, 'Shoot the other barrel, Fritz; that one missed. Your aim is rotten.' The Marines fight calmly. They take their time and keep cool."

It was not long, indeed, before our cheerful leathernecks got into the fighting, and from the first it was fighting of a daring, brilliant order. For the training period came to an end ere long and our two regiments of Marines found themselves facing the Boche across No Man's Land.

CHAPTER III

In the Trenches

WE REMAINED in the training area until March 15th and were then moved up into the line. The First Division was already in. It was composed entirely of Regular Infantry and it was that division that later saw action around Cantigny.

In March three more divisions were moved up— the 42nd, 26th, and ours. We belonged to the Second Division of the American Expeditionary Force, the 9th and 23rd Infantry comprising the Third Brigade and the Fifth and Sixth Marines, together with the Sixth Machine Gun Battalion under Major Edward B. Cole, comprising the Fourth Brigade. The division was commanded by Major General Omar Bundy of the Army.

Our officers' school at Quantico, with its one-year course, had not yet turned out enough officers for us and Army Reserve Lieutenants who had put in their application had been assigned to us. They became practically Marines in short order, some of them being killed or wounded in the subsequent fighting.

We operated under a French Brigade Commander and all our orders were in French. All our reports were at first made to this French officer and we had nothing to do with the tactical plans. We were still in training under French tutelage and remained so until May. As I have said, we had three French advisory officers assigned to each regiment—one Captain and two Lieutenants—who acted as liaison officers and kept us in touch with the French troops. Of gallant Captain Tribot-Laspierre, who was with me from the first until I fell at Belleau Wood, I shall have something to say later on.

We were sent to a sector on the heights of the Meuse southeast of Verdun. With my command I was placed in charge of a section of the trenches there. When we first went in the regiments of the Second Division were sandwiched in between French regiments, but after about a month the two regiments of Marines were brought together, side by side, as a brigade under General Doyen.

We went up by train after dark, five trains to each regiment. The German airplanes must have observed signs of activity, for the enemy began shelling the railhead. They were too late, however, for most of the men had detrained and moved away. One shell, however, did ruin the Fifth Regiment band. None of the men were hurt but the bass drum was a total wreck.

Just as we arrived at the front at midnight, a shell burst in the midst of a four-mule team. The mules were all killed and the driver was blown clean across the road, but he picked himself up uninjured. Again the human casualties were zero.

At first one battalion of each of the two regiments of Marines went into the trenches, relieving two French battalions, while the rest were held in reserve. Soon afterward a second battalion of the Sixth moved up at night to take a position in line.

The supports were located in secondary trenches about two miles back of the lines; the reserves lived in shacks and barracks above ground from three to five miles back. Some of the hardest and most dangerous work fell to the lot of the supporting units. They were kept digging trenches all the time, often under fire, and that is no child's play. Some of it was night work, and even so there were not infrequent casualties in these working parties. Our first blood was spilt in the supporting trenches when a shell killed two and wounded three men of the 82nd Company, Sixth Regiment. Such unhappy events we later became accustomed to, but I fancy there were some of our youths who, when the news of these first deaths went about, felt the sensation of a temporary quake inside, but it served only as an incentive to further effort. We knew we were in the war then, in deadly earnest, and our men drew together and faced the music with a grim determination that boded ill for the unlucky Boches who might chance to appear within range of their rifles. You may be a perfect gentleman by inheritance and training, but the sight of a dead comrade's upturned face makes you want to kill.

The first battalions in the trenches were relieved in eight days. After that the rule was twenty days

in and twenty out.   The relieved men went to the
rear to bathe and rest and have their clothes steamed,
but they were soon back digging trenches again.
There was little respite.   Digging trenches, I need
hardly remark, is a strong man's job.   It leaves the
limbs weary and the back aching.   There is about it
none of the glamour of battle, but the men knew it
was the way to whip the Hun.   One boy wrote home
that he had been reported for the first time for having
a rusty rifle.   "But," he added, "my pick and shovel
were clean and bright."   Very likely that same boy,
who had been toiling like a day labourer, caked with
dirt and sweat, had a short year before been sitting
languidly in a college classroom, clad in flossy flan-
nels, bluffing his way through a course in Greek or
Political Economy.   You can make even ditch-diggers,
and first-rate ones, out of rah-rah boys, if you can instill into them the all-pervasive spirit of the Marines.

Speaking of this trench digging, the little old mayor
of one of the villages back of our lines was heard to
remark that the war would have to last at least two
years more to give the Americans a chance to finish
their trench system.

The front line trenches at this point ran along a
ridge overlooking a plain and cut here and there by
ravines.   Behind us the country was wooded.   Both
before and behind the line there were numerous little
towns and villages, or what had once been such, a
mile or two apart.   Two or three of these, located
directly in front of our position, were used as advance
posts for observation.

Through our loopholes we looked out upon a forlorn, desolate, uninhabited country. It had passed through severe fighting in 1915, and the Germans were still shelling the woods and towns every day in the hope of getting some of our observers. The woods were splintered on every hand, the stone buildings in the villages were all knocked to pieces, and some of the open fields looked like freshly ploughed land. The whole countryside was pock-marked with craters. It was like a Doré vision of the end of the world—an abomination of desolation. Mankind and all his works appeared to have been destroyed by some devastating fire of the angry gods. It recalled burning words of Dante, Milton, Poe, Browning—these lines from "Childe Roland to the Dark Tower Came":

> I think I never saw
> Such starved, ignoble nature.
>
> . . . . .
>
> As for the grass, it grew as scant as hair
> In leprosy.
> . . . . .
>
> Then came some palsied oak, a cleft in him
> Like a distorted mouth that splits its rim
> Gaping at death, and dies while it recoils.

Yet if one could but close one's eyes to all this ghastly havoc of war, it was beautiful country, with rolling contours, a wide prospect, and wooded ridges. Spring came while we were there. The woods took on their cloak of green, and the verdant ravines, though deadly enough in all conscience, seemed to thrust themselves out into the desert plain as though trying to inject life into death. We witnessed there Nature's eternal struggle to heal her wounds.

I realize that it is not altogether easy for the civilian back home to get an accurate and vivid picture of the trenches. We occupied what is known as a "sub-sector" of the trenches that had been dug by the French. A "sub-sector" consists of a "centre of resistance," which is usually occupied by a battalion, and is made up of "strong points" which are occupied by companies. The line itself is made up of "combat groups," whose strength is according to the character of the ground. Sometimes a "combat group" consists of a non-commissioned officer and three men; sometimes there are as many as twelve men. At least half of these are alert all the time.

The trenches are not lined with men, the groups being posted at intervals of from 50 to 150 yards. At each of these posts there are men constantly on watch at loopholes in the parapet. In quiet times there is no one in the trench between these posts, and no one in the ravines, where poisonous gases may hang. The trench is not on a straight line and the whole front is covered by machine guns in such a way that a cross-fire is possible at every point. The heavier guns are placed back of the line near the support trenches, in camouflaged positions.

The support trench, which must not be confused with the position of the supporting troops farther back, is located perhaps 50 to 200 yards behind the front line and is occupied by front-line troops. It is connected with the front trench by zigzag connecting trenches. From it a main supply trench, some two miles long, runs directly back to the rear.

We had no listening posts here, owing to the width of No Man's Land at this point, but we had advance observation posts in the two villages on our front, and to these ran connecting trenches or boyaux.

The front trench where we were was merely a ditch with vertical sides, six feet deep and perhaps three feet wide or less. The main trench to the rear was wider, to permit of the passage of troops. At the best places in the front trench firing steps were cut in the front wall. Dugouts for the men not on watch were built into the earth from the rear side of the trench. They were of different sizes, some being large enough to accommodate thirty or forty men, while others were big enough for only three or four. Most of them were supplied with two entrances, so as to leave a means of exit in case of a cave-in.

Our unit had its own telephone and observation system and our signal corps men were on the jump all the time to keep it in working order. The lines were cut by shells sometimes fifteen or twenty times during the course of a day. And we had to be careful how we used our wires, for the Germans were able to steal most of our messages by means of powerful induction coils. Where we were only 100 yards from the enemy, I believe they were able to catch every word we sent along our wires, and our only safeguard was a frequent change of code.

We were in a so-called quiet sector, but quiet was

only a comparative term over there. The German artillery was active most of the time and ours replied in kind. I got my first taste of a near-by shell on the second day. I had gone down to the front trench with Captain Laspierre and we were returning through the woods together, when we heard the shrill whistle of a shell. I had already become somewhat accustomed to that whistle and then the bang of the more or less distant explosion, and it did not occur to me that this sound was any different, but the French captain's ears were in better tune. "Down!" he cried, and we jumped into a shallow ditch and lay flat. The shell struck a bare fifty feet away and burst, and the fragments rained all around us.

The French captain and I threw ourselves into the ditch five times that day while traversing half a mile. Some aviator must have signalled to the German gunners that we were there. Afterward I got so that I could quickly distinguish between the high-pitched whistle of the high velocity and the snarling shriek of the trench mortar shell. And after identifying one of the latter, one usually had between two and three seconds in which to seek the shelter of Mother Earth. Major Hughes told me that he didn't in the least mind the song of the big shells, but he did object to having tin boilers shot at him.

Every day the Germans shelled our batteries, crossroads, and camps. We were supported by French artillery at first; later American artillery came into position behind us. The 75's were placed about three-quarters of a mile back of the trenches and the 150's about two miles. They not only replied to the enemy fire but spent a good deal of time and ammunition at first in registering for barrage fire.

Boche airplanes came over nearly every day. At first, when the trees were bare, they could observe all our movements unless we executed them at night or under cover. Later on the foliage in the woods furnished us with some protection.

These trenches had originally been dug by French Colonial troops. It had been a quiet sector for two years and the trenches had not been kept in as good shape as in some places. The officers' dug-outs were in good condition, but the trenches themselves were rather bad and we had plenty of work to do to clean them out. In some spots the mud was knee-deep, and the trench dug-outs were wet. This meant discomfort and—vermin.

For the trenches are not inhabited by men alone. There were cooties and there were rats. The cootie, which is the soldier's name for a minute but very persistent member of the louse family, does not furnish a pleasant topic for conversation, but in the old trenches he is omnipresent and not at all shy and retiring in disposition. He attacks the just and the unjust, the clean and the unclean, and he is no respecter of persons. Hence the haste to bathe and get one's clothes steamed upon being relieved of trench duty. The cootie is as troublesome as shrapnel and he loves Red Cross knitting.

And the rats. They played over the men while they slept in the dug-outs. They lived and multiplied and made merry throughout the length of the trenches. They got at the reserve rations, sometimes gnawing clean through the men's packs. They were immigrants, we believed, from Germany.

There are regiments, I understand, which keep terriers for the killing of rats in the trenches. We had no terrier, but the Fifth had a mascot that was nearly as good. It was an ant bear, a sort of raccoon, which some Marine had brought from Haiti. And it did murder rats.

Dogs are used in France for various military purposes, as sentinels, couriers, ambulance assistants, etc. We had no trained dogs with our outfit, but our men were not entirely dogless. The machine gun company of the Sixth had a dog from Haiti, and one battalion owned a German shepherd dog that had been presented to it. One of the officers kept one of the rare and interesting sheepdogs of the Pyrenees.

Since I have broached the subject of dogs, let me insert a good dog story, for it has become part of the story of the Marines in France. It appeared in this form in the July 4th issue of the *Stars and Stripes*, the daily newspaper published by the American Expeditionary Force in France:

"This is the story of Verdun Belle, a trench dog who adopted a young leatherneck; of how she followed him to the edge of the battle around Château-Thierry, and was waiting for him when they carried him out. It is a true story.

"Belle is a setter bitch, shabby white, with great splotches of chocolate brown in her coat. Her ears are brown and silken. Her ancestry is dubious. She is under size, and would not stand a chance among the haughtier breeds they show in splendour at Madison Square Garden back home. But the Marines think there never was a dog like her since the world began.

"No one in the regiment knows whence she came, nor why, when she joined the outfit in a sector near Verdun, she singled out one of the privates as her very own and attached herself to him for the duration of the war. The young Marine would talk long and earnestly to her, and every one swore that Belle could 'compree' English.

"She used to curl up at his feet when he slept, or follow silently to keep him company at the listening post. She would sit hopefully in front of him whenever he settled down with his laden mess-kit, which the cooks always heaped extra high in honour of Belle.

"Belle was as used to war as the most weather-beaten poilu. The tremble of the ground did not disturb her and the whining whirr of the shells overhead only made her twitch and wrinkle her nose in her sleep. She was trench broken. You could have put a plate of savoury pork chops on the parapet and nothing would have induced her to go up after them.

"She weathered many a gas attack. Her master contrived a protection for her by cutting down and twisting a French gas mask. At first this sack over her nose irritated her tremendously, but once, when she was trying to claw it off with her forepaws, she got a whiff of the poisoned air. Then a great light dawned on Belle, and after that, at the first *alerte*, she would race for her mask. You could not have taken it from her until her master's pat on her back told her everything was all right.

"In the middle of May, Belle presented a proud but not particularly astonished regiment with nine confused and wriggling puppies, black and white or, like their mother, brown and white, and possessed of incredible appetites. Seven of these were alive and kicking when, not so very many days ago, the order came for the regiment to pull up stakes and speed across France to help stem the German tide north of the troubled Marne.

"In the rush and hubbub of marching orders, Belle and her brood were forgotten by every one but the young Marine. It never once entered his head to leave her or the pups behind. Somewhere he found a market basket and tumbled the litter into that. He could carry the pups, he explained, and the mother dog would trot at his heels.

"Now the amount of hardware a Marine is expected to carry on the march is carefully calculated to the maximum strength of the average soldier, yet this leatherneck found extra muscle somewhere for his precious basket. If it came to the worst, he thought, he could jettison his pack. It was not very clear in his mind what he would do with his charges during a battle, but he trusted to luck and Verdun Belle.

"For 40 kilometres he carried his burden along the parched French highway. No one wanted to kid him out of it nor could have if they would. When there followed a long advance by camion, he yielded his place to the basket of wriggling pups while he himself hung on the tail-board.

"But then there was more hiking and the basket proved too much. It seemed that the battle line was somewhere far off. Solemnly, the young Marine killed four of the puppies, discarded the basket, and slipped the other three into his shirt.

"Thus he trudged on his way, carrying those three, pouched in forest green, as a kangaroo carries its young, while the mother-dog trotted trustingly behind.

"One night he found that one of the black and white pups was dead. The road, by this time, was black with hurrying troops, lumbering lorries jostling the line of advancing ambulances, dust-grey columns of soldiers, moving on as far ahead and as far behind as the eye could see. Passing silently in the other direction was the desolate procession of refugees from the invaded countryside. Now and then a herd of cows or a cluster of fugitives from some desolated village, trundling their most cherished possessions in wheelbarrows and baby-carts, would cause an eddy in the traffic.

"Somewhere in this congestion and confusion Belle was lost. In the morning there was no sign of her and the young Marine did not know what to do. He begged a cup of milk from an old Frenchwoman and with the eye-dropper from his kit he tried to feed the two pups. It did not work very well. Faintly the veering wind brought down the valley from far ahead the sound of the cannon. Soon he would be in the thick of it and there was no Belle to care for the pups.

"Two ambulances of a field hospital were passing in the unending caravan. A lieutenant who looked human was in the front seat of one of them, a sergeant beside him. The leatherneck ran up to them, blurted out his story, gazed at them imploringly, and thrust the puppies into their hands.

"'Take good care of them,' he said. 'I don't suppose I'll ever see them again.'

"And he was gone. A little later in the day that field hospital was pitching its tents and setting up its kitchens and tables in a deserted farm. Amid all the hurry of preparation for the big job ahead they found time to worry about those pups. The problem was food. Corned willy was tried and found wanting.

"Finally, the first sergeant hunted up a farm-bred private, and the two of them spent that evening chasing four nervous and distrustful cows around a pasture, trying vainly to capture enough milk to provide subsistence for the new additions to the personnel.

"Next morning the problem was still unsolved. But it was solved that evening.

"For that evening a fresh contingent of Marines trooped by the farm, and in their wake—tired, anxious, but undiscouraged—was Verdun Belle. Ten kilometres back, two days before, she had lost her master, and, until she could find him again, she evidently had thought that any Marine was better than none.

"The troops did not halt at the farm, but Belle did. At the gates she stopped dead in her tracks, drew in her lolling tongue, sniffed inquiringly the evening air, and like a flash—a white streak along the drive—she raced to the distant tree where, on a pile of discarded dressings in the shade, the pups were sleeping.

"All the corps men stopped work and stood around and marvelled. For the onlooker it was such a family reunion as warms the heart. For the worried mess sergeant it was a great relief. For the pups it was a mess call, clear and unmistakable.

"So, with renewed faith in her heart and only one worry left in her mind, Verdun Belle and her puppies settled down to detached service with this field hospital. When, next day, the reach of the artillery made it advisable that it should move down the valley to the shelter of a fine hillside château, you may be sure that room was made in the first ambulance for the three casuals.

"In a grove of trees beside the house, the tents of the personnel were pitched and the cots of the expected patients ranged side by side. The wounded came—came hour after hour in a steady stream, and the boys of the hospital worked on them night and day. They could not possibly keep track of all the cases, but there was one who did. Always a mistress of the art of keeping out from under foot, very quietly Belle hung around and investigated each ambulance that turned in from the main road and backed up with its load of pain to the door of the receiving room.

"Then one evening they lifted out a young Marine, listless in the half stupour of shell shock. To the busy workers he was just Case Number Such-and-Such, but there was no need to tell any one who saw the wild jubilance of the dog that Belle had found her own again at last.

"The first consciousness he had of his new surroundings was the feel of her rough, pink tongue licking the dust from his face. And those who passed that way on Sunday last found two cots shoved together in the kindly shade of a spreading tree. On one the mother-dog lay contented with her puppies. Fast asleep on the other, his arm thrown out so that the grimy hand could clutch one silken ear, lay the young Marine.

"Before long they would have to ship him to the evacuation hospital, on from there to the base hospital, on and on and on. It was not very clear to any one how another separation could be prevented. It was a perplexing question. But they knew in their hearts they could safely leave the answer to some one else. They could leave it to Verdun Belle."

CHAPTER IV

Over the Top

OUTSIDE of the artillery fire and repelling a few minor German raids, nothing very exciting happened at first. Then we began sending patrols every night into No Man's Land, and the real danger and uncertainty of trench warfare began for our Marines—and the longed-for chance for action.

These patrols were divided into two classes—wire patrols, which went over the top to cut German wire entanglements and to look after the condition of ours, and reconnoitring patrols which stole out in search of information. Neither of these was a raiding party, though a German prisoner or two was always welcome.

The reconnoitring patrols were sent out with a definite route to follow and a definite time schedule. This schedule was handed to the artillery, which was ready with a barrage in case an enemy raid was signalled. Obviously, it was important for the patrol to stick to its route and schedule so as to be in no danger from our own barrage.

The average patrol numbered not less than twenty-five men under a commissioned officer. The German patrols were usually a bit larger—about forty men.

There was always the possibility of running upon an enemy patrol, and that meant quick action and a bloody fight.

Perhaps it requires more nerve to steal out in the night in this way, creeping over the top and skulking along Indian fashion, with no way of knowing how many Germans may be in the path, than to advance into battle in regular formation in broad daylight. But our Marines took to it as though it were the best game ever invented, and I have no doubt it helped to fit them for what came later.

Clashes with German patrols were frequent. They became a part of the night's work, these unearthly encounters in the dread dark, and our Marines learned to take the hazard and fight the unseen. Quietly they would steal over the top like boys embarking on some exciting game, and then comparative silence would reign in the trenches while we waited for the patrol to come back. It was filled with suspense, that waiting, for the crack of a rifle out there in No Man's Land, or the bursting of a grenade might mean the snuffing out of another young American life, and another Marine reported dead or missing. Often there was a pitched battle beneath the stars, and when the boys came in again they had a tale to tell of fleeing Germans or dead foes hanging on the wire.

I remember one occasion in which a party of thirty men of the Fifth went over into No Man's Land in the dead of night on their stealthy, dangerous mission. One of the Army Reserve Lieutenants, a Plattsburgh graduate named A. L. Sundeval, attached to the 18th Company, was in command of the patrol. Deploying as much as was safe in the darkness, they made their way over the shell holes and entanglements until suddenly the thirty ran head on into a large German patrol numbering at least a hundred men. But the Marine does not count his enemy's numbers. Without a moment's hesitation battle was joined there in the darkness, which was made even more intense by occasional flares and star shells in the distance. Rifles cracked and spat fire, and now and then a grunt told of an American bayonet that had found its sheath in a German body. The conflict ebbed and flowed out there between two inactive armies, with no one to watch its progress, but our Marines fought the Boches to a standstill, and when the enemy at last turned and disappeared in the darkness they carried with them a new respect for the fighting of the devil hounds and left behind their slain.

When it was all over, and the boys came back, Lieutenant Sundeval was lying motionless on the ground and two men were reported missing. A gunnery sergeant of the 18th Company named Winchenbaugh, a loyal son of Poland, picked up the dying Lieutenant and brought him in under fire. For that he received the Croix de Guerre and was recommended for the Distinguished Service Cross.

Such were the adventures of our patrols out there in the wire-entangled waste of No Man's Land when the night was black and every man carried his life in his hands. Great battles and the movements of huge armies under illustrious generals crowd the reports of such deeds from the newspapers, but they are the deeds of brave men, fighting and dying in France for the great cause. And out there in No Man's Land the Hun took bloody toll of our Marines, but he paid the price.

More spectacular than the patrol work, perhaps, were the raids which were made on the enemy's trenches for the purpose of securing prisoners and direct information. The Germans were also addicted to the habit of raiding, and we had some lively times repelling their raids. They were seldom successful. On one occasion they attempted a raid on a battalion of the Fifth during relief, and left behind them two prisoners and three dead.

As the days went by and our men stiffened to their work, there were stirring events for the Marines. They became more skilful in their night patrol work, bolder in their raids, more stubborn in their resistance of the enemy's dashes.

I have spoken of the little demolished villages in front of our lines which we used as advance observation posts. The squads in these outposts were practically isolated part of the time. Each advance post was reached by a single connecting trench or boyau which was wide open to the enemy's fire and could be used only under cover of darkness. The Germans shelled these villages every day and the men were obliged to make dugouts. They did most of their sleeping in the daytime and remained watchful all night.

In one of these posts we had fifty men under one officer, Lieutenant Perkinson. No Man's Land at this point was about three quarters of a mile wide, but it was not a safe spot night or day. Eternal watchfulness was the price of life.

One night, at 11.30, we heard the roar of the barrage and the rattle of machine guns and learned that a raid was being made on this post. The story of that raid, as it was afterward told me, was dramatic. The German patrols had succeeded in cutting all but the last line of wire without being detected. It was a night of velvet blackness and our men were on the alert. Out of the stillness of No Man's Land—for there is a sort of comparative stillness there—there came to the ears of our listeners the sharp snap of wire cutters near at hand. The Germans were at work on the last line of barbed wire.

The word was quickly passed along and the automatic rifles blazed out. The Germans replied with such vigour and volume that our men at once recognized it for a raid in force. They were clearly outnumbered, though it was impossible for them to tell just how great their peril was. They kept their automatics going, but the Germans refused to be beaten back. Help was imperatively needed.

Lieutenant Perkinson ordered his men to signal to our artillery for a barrage, but the rockets had become damp and refused to go off. The situation was serious for that little band of Marines. Then two men—Privates Sleeth and Hullinger—volunteered to go back to the first line trench for a fresh supply of rockets. Sleeth was a ten-second sprinter, and the two started back by the shell-torn road, as the winding boyau offered too great an impediment to speed and was not much safer at night.

When our rifles spoke, the Germans knew there was no further need for stealth and they signalled back to their gunners for a barrage to prevent reinforcements from being sent to our men. As our two runners started out on their dash up the slope, this barrage was being methodically laid down right across the boyau and the strip of ground lying between our front line trench and the advance post. The runners had to make their way directly through this curtain of shell fire and return the same way.

Now an artillery barrage is a pretty effective check to advancing troops, but a single man may hope, with luck, to get through with a whole skin. The German shells were dropped frequently and accurately at a range of about 3,000 yards, falling to earth about twenty to thirty feet apart. This is too close for comfort, and a man's only hope is to get through in the interval between two shots from the same guns.

Our runners had their wits about them and they made their calculations. Both of them got through by a miracle, though Hullinger fell exhausted when he reached the shelter of the trench. The sprinter came loping back to us with an armful of rockets, beating the barrage on his return. Picture to yourself that wild midnight dash through a hell of bursting shells, and you will have some idea of the sort of deeds our new Marines were proving themselves capable of.

As it turned out, those rockets were not needed, after all, for Lieutenant Perkinson and his men beat the Germans back without the aid of a barrage. It was the incessant argument of their rifles that persuaded the Boches to retire from their ill-starred venture. It was pitch-dark, and the men could see neither their victims nor the sights on their rifles. But they knew how to shoot low and to fire at a sound or a flash, and their fire proved effective. The Germans evidently did not like this form of death in the dark, for it was not long before they had had enough. They threw over a volley of grenades and departed. The German barrage kept up for half an hour longer, as if for spite, and then quieted down.

About daylight small patrols were sent out to investigate. They found two dead Huns, besides spots of blood and other signs of numerous casualties. They also picked up about 500 hand grenades, fifty big two-handed wire cutters, and a quantity of tubes of liquid fire which the Germans had dropped in their hasty retreat. Their little undertaking had proved a bit costly for them, but the fight might easily have gone the other way, for they had succeeded in cutting half through the last entanglement and were close upon our post when they were detected. From the evidence gathered it was estimated that they must have outnumbered the fifty Americans more than two to one.

As for the Marines in that action, not one was killed and only one man wounded, and he by shrapnel at the beginning of the German barrage. He received seven separate wounds, but he crawled to his position and stuck there throughout the engagement. Lieutenant Perkinson received the Croix de Guerre for that night's work, and so did the two runners.

There was one other little affair which had its heroic moments. In another of the little towns at the foot of the hill, where the lines were about 1,000 yards apart, we kept two platoons—100 men. One night a combination patrol started out from this post, consisting of equal numbers of French and Americans, the latter under Lieutenant Burr. Again it was midnight and dark as a pocket. They had got about 200 yards outside the lines when they ran headlong into a party of Germans who were evidently planning a raid on the advance post. The Germans, not knowing just what they were up against, turned and fled.

In about two minutes a signal went up and a German barrage was laid down between the Allied patrol and the town. Eight batteries of four guns each poured in a perfect torrent of explosive shells and the retreat of our men was effectively cut off. As the barrage crept nearer they scuttled for shell holes and ditches and lay there waiting for the storm to subside.

Next morning four dead Germans were found near the town, killed by their own barrage. One Marine was killed that night—Corporal Toth. They found him the following day, sitting in a ditch with a machine gun bullet in his head.

And so we left our dead in No Man's Land, and we loved the Hun no more for that.

On the whole, I am inclined to think that the gas was the worst evil we had to encounter, and we learned to dread the deadly smell of mustard. One whole company of the Sixth got it once and got it bad. It was the 74th, under Captain Miller, which was in reserve, living in barracks in a ravine back of the lines. One morning an intense bombardment of this camp broke loose, and between 4 and 6 A. M. over 2,000 gas shells fell. Thirty-nine of our men were killed during that bombardment or died from the effects of it, and others were seriously gassed. They were caught before reveille, as they supposed in a safe retreat, and the damage was done before a warning could be given and the masks adjusted. One of the first shells went through the roof of a hut where sixty men were sleeping, and most of the thirty-nine killed were in that platoon.

On the same day the Germans bombarded another camp with gas and inflicted casualties. The Boche must certainly be given credit for knowing how to use gas and for his cleverness in getting it over without warning. Later gas was mixed with explosives and you couldn't tell a gas shell from any other by the sound or look of it.

During those days and nights in the trenches the Quartermaster's outfit had as hard a time of it as any of us. Hard work and little glory was their lot, but they stood to their task like men and the boys in front were fed. The supply company was located three miles in the rear and every twenty-four hours the commissary detachments had to get adequate supplies to the battalion dumps at the front whether the roads were shelled or not. It all had to be done at night and the weather had no place in the calculations. Food was taken to the front line every night by the battalion Quartermaster and his men on mule carts, pack mules, etc., as well as timber, wire, camouflage, and all the other material and paraphernalia of trench warfare. The Germans had the roads registered and dropped shells on them at intervals during the night. The time schedule of the supply trains was changed frequently, but even so the shells not infrequently got them, and the casualties steadily increased. But night after night they had to keep going through the peril of it, and there is none of the excitement and uplift of battle in driving mules at night.

We remained in this sub-sector one month and then traded positions with a French regiment. This placed the Sixth next to the Fifth and brought our brigade of Marines together in the region of Les Eparges. At this new position of the Sixth the woods jutted farther out upon the plain, and at one point the opposing trenches were only 150 yards apart. Here we had listening posts in the old French trench just outside our first line of wire.

I had been living more or less comfortably in an

old dugout back of our former line. Now I moved my Post of Command to a point near a high hill overlooking the new lines. This hill was the site of an ancient Roman camp of which the earthworks were still visible. A grass-grown mound ten feet high ran across the hill, telling of military undertakings of a by-gone day. My new post was consequently named P. C. Rome.

It was here that I experienced my second personal encounter with Boche shells. About ten o'clock one morning, soon after I had taken up my post there, the Germans began bombarding the camp of the headquarters company near at hand, killing three men and wounding two. Rafales of twenty shells were fired into the camp at intervals of twenty minutes all day, but fortunately for me none of them struck the Post of Command.

During the month that we remained in this position, the Sixth had no actual contact with the Germans, though the French had twice been raided there just before we came. Patrol work, however, went steadily on. One night an unlucky patrol stumbled into a cleverly placed trip wire which exploded grenades when it was struck and caught the men in the legs. Several were wounded, including Lieutenant Wallace, one of my battalion intelligence officers.

That same night one of our companies was gassed, but we knew more about gas and gas masks by that time. A few gas shells fell near the Post of Command, and I had my mask on. Toward morning I heard a bird singing in a tree near by. It struck me that if there wasn't enough gas in the air to kill a bird, it wouldn't kill me, and I took off the mask.

A gas mask, by the way, is a thing one is anxious to take off at the first opportunity. It is a hot and stifling thing and seems to impede the faculties. The wearer takes in the air through his mouth, after it has been sucked through the purifying chemicals. His nose is not trusted and is clamped shut. Imagine yourself fighting with a clothespin on your nose and a bag over your mouth and you may be able to get some notion of what a gas mask is like. And at that it is preferable to one whiff of the deadly fumes.

Spring advanced and May came. Verdure overspread the old Roman camp on the hill. Wild flowers burst into bloom and birds sang in the woods. I remember coming upon a hillside that was white and fragrant with a great mass of lily-of-the-valley. On the plain below the shell-ploughed farms clothed themselves in green sprinkled with wild flowers. At another time and under other circumstances it would have been a peaceful, restful scene.

It was on one of these bright days in May that we assembled in a wooded spot back of the lines at 10 o'clock in the morning to witness the decoration of our heroes. There under the trees those of our men who had won especial honour received from a grateful and appreciative Ally their hard-earned recognition —the coveted Croix de Guerre.

The recipients, numbering about twenty-five American Marines and about the same number of French soldiers in that sector, were drawn up inside a hollow square composed of two companies of French troops and two of Marines. A French band rendered martial music and a number of high French officials filed in. It was an impressive ceremony. One by one the citations were read, giving a résumé of each man's deeds of valour and service, there was a burst of bugle notes, and the Cross was pinned on and the Gallic salutation administered by General Tenant of the French Army. In that simple ceremony and in the knowledge of what it meant, our men found their reward for all the perils and labours they had undergone in No Man's Land and the trenches.

Early in May, shortly before we left the trenches, General Doyen, on account of ill health, was relieved of his command of the brigade by Brigadier General Harbord of the Army. Of course we were a bit disappointed not to have a Marine officer at our head, but there was no Brigadier General of Marines in France at that time, and it was advisable to have an officer of that rank in command of the brigade. But every Marine in the brigade knew that a better man could not have been assigned to the post. General Harbord had been General Pershing's Chief of Staff; the very best had been sent to us, and that we appreciated.

General Harbord was a splendid soldier. I had known him as a member of my class at the War College. He was first of all a man of action, and from the time he took over our force in the trenches things were always on the move. He was a glutton for work himself and was always inspecting something or somebody. There were no idle units under him. And he exhibited that ideal combination of discipline and the democratic attitude which we like to think is typically American. He was popular with the men, talked with them often, and obviously had their interests at heart. Marines to him were something more than cannon fodder, and the men knew it and worked their hardest for him. It is impossible to overestimate the value of such officers with our boys in France.

Though not a Marine himself, General Harbord fully understood and appreciated the traditions of our Corps, and it was said of him that he became as pro-Marine as any Marine. He told us that when he took over the command, General Pershing said to him, "You are to have charge of the finest body of troops in France, and if they fail to live up to that reputation I shall know whom to blame." That they did live up to their reputation necessarily throws not a little credit upon their commander.

I speak of these things because General Harbord was our commanding officer during all the stirring days that followed. Our orders all came from him and he handled the brigade of Marines at Belleau Wood and Bouresches. After that action he was made a Major General, and he deserved it.

I cannot refrain from adding a few words here regarding General Doyen, the first commander of our brigade, for he has given his life to the service as truly as if he had been killed by a German bullet.

He was born in Concord, N. H., on September 3, 1859, and was admitted to the Naval Academy as midshipman in June, 1876.   He graduated with the Class of 1881 and received his commission as Second Lieutenant in the Marine Corps in 1883.   He saw service in all parts of the world with the Atlantic and Pacific Fleets.   He was made First Lieutenant in 1889, Captain in 1898, and Major in 1900, when he was assigned to the command of the Marines of the Atlantic Fleet.   In 1905 he became a Lieutenant Colonel and took command of the Marines then in the Philippines.   He received his Colonel's commission in 1909 and went to the Philippines again in 1913.   In 1915 he was assigned to the command of the Marine Barracks at Washington, D. C.

When the United States went into the war, Colonel Doyen was the officer selected to command the first brigade of Marines to be sent to France.   Under him our two regiments underwent the months of vigorous training on French soil that fitted them for the service which they saw later.   Full credit should be given him for that.   When we went into the trenches he was relieved of his command because of ill health.   He was made a Brigadier General to date from March 26, 1917.

On his return to this country he was placed in command of the Marine Barracks and Overseas Training Station at Quantico, Va., and died there of influenza on October 6, 1918.   His death was a great loss to the service.   He was a fine type of officer, one of the most distinguished in our Corps, and embodied all of those traditions of which we are so proud.

It was while we were in the trenches, in that "quiet" sector, that the terrible, heart-sickening drive of the Germans in Picardy was going on. Rheims was threatened, and the Boches plunged steadily on toward Amiens, across the Somme, through Peronne, and down to Montdidier. It was almost more than flesh and blood could stand to lie there in our dugouts and learn what was going on to the northwest. Every man of us knew all about it, for we picked up the German and French communiqués by wireless. The former were the most disquieting, for, with characteristic exaggeration, they told of tremendous victories and whole armies taken prisoner. We did not know then, as we know now, that the German invariably lies in his communiqués. The French and British do not lie, though they are often obliged, for military reasons, to conceal the precise extent of their losses during important actions.

Naturally we began to grow restless. Why could we take no part in this crucial action? Why weren't the American Marines called upon to help stem the fiery tide that seemed to be sweeping so irresistibly onward? We learned that the First Division had been sent in at Cantigny, and this did not add to our contentment. For a month we looked for orders to move, but none came.

At last, in the second week of May, the orders came. We were to proceed to a rest area on May 14th, after having been in the trenches exactly two months. We rejoiced, for the order meant a rest from trench digging, relief from the nightly peril of No Man's Land, a fond farewell to the mud and rats and cooties. But it meant more than that; it meant the likelihood of our being prepared for action on the battle line. We felt that our initiation had been completed, that at last we belonged, that we were now an intrinsic part of the Allied armies in France that were fighting so desperately in the common cause of human justice and liberty.

A new ardour seemed to possess the men when the news of that order went the rounds. Eagerly we climbed out of the damp and narrow trenches, fought one more battle with the cooties, and looked for the last time on "the misty mid-region of Wier" which was No Man's Land. And behind us we left slain comrades; that we did not forget.

CHAPTER V

THE DRIVE THAT MENACED PARIS

ON MAY 14th we were withdrawn to a rest
area in the rear of the lines where we remained for five days. Then we were ordered
to still another one to the northwest of Paris. We
skirted the city on our way, but none of the men were
given leave and we were obliged to sigh regretfully
and pass on.

In this second rest area we remained till the end
of May. We rested, or at least it seemed like rest to
the boys who were weary with the nerve-racking
grind of trench work, but General Harbord did not
believe in idleness. There was constant police work
and constant drilling. And there we reformed our
units for the task ahead of us, and overhauled our
equipment.

It may perhaps be interesting to enumerate some
of the things which a regiment of Marines in France
has to carry about with it and keep in condition.
Each man, of course, had his personal effects, weigh-
ing in all about sixty pounds, which he was obliged
to carry when travelling in heavy marching order.
There was the Colonel's automobile and fifty-nine
riding horses for the officers, all of which had to be
kept in perfect condition by the men. The auto-

mobile went to the front, but the horses were not much in evidence in the front lines.

Our medical service was attached to the division. It was taken from the Navy force and included nine medical officers and forty enlisted men. That they had plenty to do will be evident later.

Each regiment had three motor cycles with side cars for messenger service, though in the press of battle runners had to be depended upon. Then there was all the paraphernalia of telephone and signal service, the ammunition, and all the adjuncts of fighting. The baggage wagons, ration wagons, water carts, ammunition wagons, rolling kitchens, etc., were all drawn by mules, as was our complement of machine guns. We used the heavy Hotchkiss. There were 332 mules, in all, attached to our regiment, and they, of course, had to be cared for.

And then there was Lizzie. She was a Ford car presented by Miss Elizabeth Pearce of New York to the Marine Corps for service with the Sixth Regiment. She was equipped as an ambulance and was used as such in Bordeaux, when our camp was five miles outside the city. When we joined the rest of the Second Division, the regular ambulance service of the division supplied all our needs in that direction.

But don't think for a moment that Lizzie was discarded. I believe there was no more useful member in the whole regiment. She was first pressed into service as a mail carrier to and from Division Headquarters. When we got to the trenches I hardly know what she was not used for. She was the rapid transit system for the regiment in the front lines. Up there in the trench sector she met with a bad accident. Somehow she got smashed up in a ditch and the ambulance top was lost. She looked like a total wreck, but the good old engine still ran. The boys got her out of the ditch, cleaned up the wreckage, and converted her into a sort of open delivery truck. And all through those weeks in the trenches she rendered invaluable service.

I don't know how thoroughly she was overhauled during our rest period, but I believe she made no complaint of neglect. When at last we got to the fighting front, Lizzie came through with the supply train on June 4th. She was used almost constantly, especially after June 6th, to carry ammunition and food to the front lines, and the boys had many an occasion to rise up and call her blessed. She proved to be, in a way, our guardian angel.

She was still in commission the last I knew. One wheel wabbled and she was full of shrapnel holes, but still she ran. And the men had painted a large Croix de Guerre on the side of her hood.

Already Lizzie has inspired the muse of at least one poet. The following verses, written by Wallace Irwin for the Marines, are printed here with the author's permission.

ELIZABETH FORD

We carried her over the sea, we did,
  And taught her to hep, hep, hep—
A cute little jinny, all noisy and tinny,
  But full of American pep.

Recruited into the Corps she was—
　　She came of her own accord.
We flew at her spanker the globe and the anchor
　　And named her Elizabeth Ford.

'Cute little 'Lizabeth, dear little 'Lizabeth,
　　Bonnie Elizabeth Ford!
She was short and squat, but her nose was sot
　　For the Hindenburg line—O Lord!
She hated a Hun like a son-of-a-gun,
　　The Kaiser she plumb abhorred,
Did chunky Elizabeth, hunky Elizabeth,
　　Spunky Elizabeth Ford.

We took her along on our hikes, we did,
　　And a wonderful boat was she.
She'd carry physicians, food or munitions,
　　Generals, water, or tea.
She could climb a bank like a first-rate tank
　　And deliver the goods aboard—
When we touch our steel Kellies to "Semper Fidelis,"
　　Remember Elizabeth Ford.

'Cute little 'Lizabeth, dear little 'Lizabeth,
　　Bonnie Elizabeth Ford.
She took her rests in machine gun nests
　　And on bullet-swept roads she chored.
Where the Devil Hounds were first on the grounds
　　Of a section of France restored—
Why, there was Elizabeth, chunky Elizabeth,
　　Spunky Elizabeth Ford!

But 'twas on the day at those murder-woods
　　Which the Yankees pronounce Belloo;

We were sent to knock silly the hopes of Prince Willie
  And turn 'em around d. q.
We prayed for munitions and cleared our throats
  With a waterless click—good Lord!—
When out of a crater with bent radiator
  Climbed faithful Elizabeth Ford!

'Cute little 'Lizabeth, dear little 'Lizabeth,
  Bonnie Elizabeth Ford.
With a cylinder-skip she had made the trip,
  Water-and-cartridge-stored.
With her hood a wreck and a broken neck
  She cracked like a rotten board.
Hunky Elizabeth, chunky Elizabeth,
  Spunky Elizabeth Ford.

When they towed her out of the town next day
  Said Corporal Bill, "Look there!
I know of one hero who shouldn't draw zero
  When they're passin' the Croix de Guerre.
Who fed the guns that's startin' the Huns
  Plumb back to Canal du Nord?"
So his Cross—and he'd won it!—he tied to the bonnet
  Of faithful Elizabeth Ford.

'Cute little 'Lizabeth, dear little 'Lizabeth,
  Bonnie Elizabeth Ford!
Where shrapnel has mauled her we've now overhauled her,
  Her wheels and her gears restored.
Her record's clean, she's a true Marine
  And we're sending the Dutch War Lord
A note by Elizabeth, chunky Elizabeth,
  Spunky Elizabeth Ford!

In the rest area we were rather more pleasantly located than in our previous training area. At least it seemed so, for the dreary winter weather was over and spring was at its height. The little villages in which we were billeted looked very pretty, with their gardens and neat houses, and we tried to keep them so. Part of our police work consisted in raking the streets and roads by hand and keeping the whole place shipshape.

Unquestionably the men were benefited by the change. Complete relaxation, however, was out of the question, for we knew how things were going with our Allies and we lived from day to day expecting, and hoping for, the call that came at last.

Before telling of our response to that call, of how we went to the hard-pressed front and joined battle with the victorious Hun, it might be well to set the stage by reviewing the military situation as it then existed.

It will be recalled that the first spring drive of the Germans started on March 21st, 1918. Across the Somme it swept, engulfing the plains of Picardy in a huge wedge, and carrying discouragement to the hearts of the Allied nations. Foch was at the helm at last, but he seemed unable to check the advance. Amiens was threatened, and there were wild speculations of a rush to the sea and the separation of the French from the British. Men asked where the Allied army of manœuvre could be, and Foch answered not.

Over there in the trenches we realized these things

and we were anxious and restless. So was everybody. I now believe that General Foch was the wisest and most patient man in France. He bided his time, and at last the onsweeping tide spent its force and the Allied lines were reformed. The drive was checked and counter-attacks began. The First Division of the American Army was sent in, and it will be remembered that it was American troops of that division that stormed and captured Cantigny, northwest of Montdidier, on May 28th. The Marines, you may well believe, envied those lucky troops, but our turn was to come soon enough.

The Hun, however, had by no means expended all his long stored strength. The drive in Picardy having reached its limit, and the Ypres and Arras barriers holding in the north, it was inevitable that Ludendorff should feel out another spot to break through farther south. His railroad and concentration facilities were excellent and the Crown Prince was begging for a chance to retrieve his vast failure at Verdun.

The line northwest of Rheims was the logical point, but Foch, though he probably saw this, was still obliged to concentrate his army of manœuvre in Picardy, and the weary forces in the Champagne were unable to withstand the power of the new drive. This had been a quiet portion of the line for a year and was not strongly held. The French, weakened and surprised, were forced to fall back.

The German struck hard and suddenly. The new drive started on May 27th, while we were in the rest area, and it was with consternation that we watched the ease with which the enemy carried the Chemin des Dames and the Aisne near fortified Soissons.   Both natural and human barriers seemed to crumble before them.

Possibly Foch was for the moment outgeneralled, being deceived by feints to the north.   Perhaps it was all a part of his far-sighted plan to let the enemy wear himself down by extreme efforts.   At any rate, on they came, sweeping everything before them, demoralizing the French army opposed to them, and heading straight for the Paris of their dreams.   We realized that with a sinking of the heart; Paris realized it; everybody realized it; but what was to be done?   The Metz-to-Paris road was definitely threatened, but what barrier was there to throw across their path?   And we, lying in our pleasant billets, could only curse and wait.

With forty divisions, including some 400,000 of their best troops, and with the greatest auxiliary force of tanks, machine guns, and poison gas projectors ever mobilized, they rolled on for thirty miles, in spite of enormous losses, advancing at the rate of six or eight miles a day, capturing men and guns by the wholesale, and occupying 650 square miles of territory.   There were simply not enough French and British there to stop them.   The Allies resisted heroically, but they were forced to yield to the unanswerable argument of superior weight.   And where was that American aid that the French people had been building their failing hopes upon?

An unfathomable gloom and depression settled over weary France—the numbness of utter despair.

An uncanny sense of disaster and impending doom oppressed us all. It was a dark moment for the Allied cause.

Held at Rheims and west of Soissons, the Germans thrust a U-shaped salient clear down to the Marne, its rounded apex resting on a contracted six-mile front between Château-Thierry and Dormans, but thirty-five scant miles from Paris.

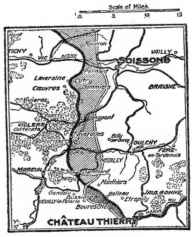

DIAGRAM 1

This map shows the western side and southern extremity of the salient created by the German drive of May, 1918. Chateau-Thierry, on the Marne, is only thirty-five miles from Paris. The heavily shaded section northwest of Chateau-Thierry is the ground won back by the American Second Division after June 6th.

Then the harried soldiers of France arose in their might for a last grim stand. The name of the Marne was a rallying cry for them. "They shall not pass," they muttered between gritted teeth, and they did not pass. There behind the prepared defences of the Marne the French line held at last, and the German hordes, having outrun their artillery, met with a check. Oh, the glory of that stand! It will live in the hearts of the French people forever.

But the Hun was not through. He had plenty

of men to bring up, plenty of guns. They might still have turned the trick if the unexpected had not happened to upset their calculations. On June 1st and 2nd the Germans made a determined effort to broaden the point of the salient northwest of Château-Thierry and to find a weak spot to break through, and it was here that they met with a new and by them entirely unforeseen element of resistance. The Yanks had come at last.

There was a weak spot there, a gap to be plugged, one of the most dangerous points on the whole front. Very likely Foch was not yet quite ready to use the American troops, but the emergency was acute. The Second Division of the American Army was thrown in in a final effort to defend the Metz-to-Paris road and save the city.

The Germans, who had become accustomed to the weakening resistance of the French, did not know what to make of it at first. But they soon learned the taste of American mettle and metal. They were stopped in their overwhelming rush, and stopped for good. Between June 6th and 12th they were fought to a standstill on that narrow front, the best of the Kaiser's vanguard troops, flushed with victory as they were. And not only stopped; the bow of the salient between La Feste-Milon and Château-Thierry was actually bent back.

Unquestionably, Paris had been in deadly peril. There had seemed little chance of preventing the Germans from sweeping around west of Château-Thierry and across the Marne. But they couldn't

do it. The United States Marines wouldn't let them.
We plugged that gap, we held that line, and the
German was stopped then and there.

As the inspired Berlin *Vossische Zeitung* put it,
"The German Supreme Command cannot well

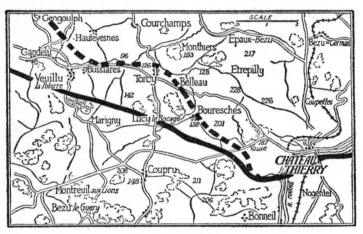

DIAGRAM 2

The territory between the two heavy lines was won back in June, 1918, by American
soldiers and Marines of the Second Division. The Bois de Belleau lies in the center of
the map, west of Bouresches and northeast of Lucy-le-Bocage.

proceed now against the newly consolidated French
front, which is richly provided with reserves, and
bear the great losses which experience shows are
entailed by such operations." The chief of the
reserves with which the French were so "richly provided" were two regiments of American Marines.

That was the military situation in early June, 1918.
How the Marines turned the tide of battle there is
the tale I have to tell.

Meanwhile, however, there were preliminary actions which should be mentioned, for there were Americans, though not Marines, who stood shoulder to shoulder with the heroic French when they made their glorious stand at Château-Thierry.

The first contingent of Americans to arrive at this crucial moment was a unit of machine gunners—one battalion of the Third Division with forty-eight guns. On May 31st, when the capture of the town of Château-Thierry by the Germans was imminent, they arrived in the nick of time.

This was, as a matter of fact, one of the tensest and most critical moments of the war, for if the Germans had broken through at Château-Thierry and had thrown their vanguard across the Marne, it is difficult to see how anything could have stopped them before they reached the defences of Paris. The delay occasioned by the stubborn resistance of the French and Americans at Château-Thierry gave us a chance to organize the defensive strategy which culminated in the battle of Belleau Wood and the thrusting back of the German hordes.

The city of Château-Thierry is built on both banks of the Marne, and by the time the Americans arrived the Germans had beaten down the French defence north of the town, had pushed their way in, and had established positions on the northern bank of the river. They dominated the bridges with their guns, and the battered French, forming for a last desperate stand on the southern bank, had but a slight chance of preventing a crossing in force.

The Germans believed they were going to push straight through to Paris. They came in ever increasing numbers, gaily goose-stepping down the roads to Château-Thierry, in columns of fours, with their rifles on their shoulders, singing. There were many on both sides who said, "Well, the war is over." It looked like a mere matter of marching to the Germans.

At the bridgeheads they paused to form for the final assault that was to sweep the French out of the town—and they paused a moment too long. From the southeast a small but irresistible whirlwind blew into Château-Thierry—a sort of Kansas cyclone— and it hit the bewildered Boche square in the face.

When the Germans were reported to be in the outskirts of the town a hurried and despairing call for help went out—any help at all, so that it came quickly. Some 100 kilometres to the rear was stationed an American machine gun battalion that was ready and eager for battle but was waiting for the fuller organization of the Third Division. But this was no time for waiting. The battalion was ordered in without support and made a speedy all-night trip to the front on motor lorries.

These boys had never faced German shell fire before; they were stiff and cramped after their long night ride; but the smell of powder and the roar of combat were like wine to them and they jumped into the thick of the fray like veterans. Joining a battalion of French Colonials, they entered the town and rushed to the threatened bank of the river.

There were dash and fury in that American charge, but there was coolness, too. Under a galling fire to which they were unaccustomed they brought up their guns and organized their defence positions at the bridges with mathematical precision.

Then came the Germans, a long, grey flood of them, streaming down to the bridges. The Americans opened upon them a fire so furious and accurate that the advancing columns hesitated, wavered, and then halted behind the barrier of their fallen comrades. Then they came on again.

On the bridges and in the streets of Château-Thierry there raged a wild, demoniacal tempest of machine gun and rifle fire. The enemy, infuriated by this resistance, fought desperately to brush the offensive Yankees from their path. Our boys fell by the dozens beside their guns, but there was always some one to leap into the breach and keep the stream of bullets pouring into the ranks of the thwarted Huns. They held the southern bank of the Marne against the onslaught; they cleared the bridges; and at last they destroyed them, and the Germans could not pass. They repulsed the enemy at every point and they helped the French to keep their vow.

Never have men fought with greater heroism, dash, and gallantry under the American flag than did those machine gunners of the lone battalion at Château-Thierry. They fell, dead and wounded, many of them, but not one was taken prisoner, though they captured a number of Germans as well as machine guns.

The Germans held the northern part of the town until the Allied offensive of July 18th and 19th, when they withdrew before Franco-American pressure, but they never once gained a foothold in the part of the city lying to the south of the Marne.

We Marines have a special interest in that engagement, apart from the fact that it was an American exploit. The officer in command of that battalion of machine gunners happened to be a Major of Marines, who had been sent to them for training. He was, in fact, the son of our own beloved General Waller, who was himself unable to go to France, having been in command of the Advance Base Brigade at Philadelphia since the affair in Haiti.

When our own Second Division went in, after the manner which I shall presently describe, it was the 23rd Infantry which saw the first action. On June 1st they beat off two determined German attacks on the Marne. The enemy had concentrated large forces before Veuilly Wood and began a mass attack, seeking to penetrate the wood. The advancing German phalanx was mowed down by our machine guns and the attack was broken up before it reached the American line. Then, by a magnificent counterattack, the Hun was hurled back.

An enemy battalion which crept across the Marne to the left bank above Jaulgonne was counterattacked by French and Americans and was thrown back to the other bank with losses. After that the Allies held the Marne.

I have mentioned these engagements in order that

full justice may be done, for I have no wish to dim the glory of the Infantry by dwelling solely on the achievements of the Marines. The Marines won glory enough in the days that followed, and it is their story that I shall now narrate.

PART II

FIGHTING TO SAVE PARIS

CHAPTER VI

GOING IN

A T LAST the great call came. We left our
rest area on the morning of May 31st and
took our places in the battle line on the
afternoon of June 1st. And the hours between were
packed with action.

The drive into Picardy had been stopped, it will
be remembered, and the First Division had been
fighting there. We were located not much over
fifty miles from Montdidier, and we were fully expecting to be sent up back of Cantigny to relieve the
First Division. We did, in fact, receive orders to
be ready to leave for the Beauvais district on the
morning of May 31st, and on the morning of the
30th we sent our billeting officers up there to arrange
our quarters.

Then came the sudden, acute crisis at Château-
Thierry, and the plans of the High Command were
hastily changed. When the orders failed to come
we suspected what it meant. We had been reading
the Paris papers and we knew the situation. I believe there was not a man in my regiment whose
hopes were not raised by the delay in the orders.
Our Marines were in fine shape for action, and they

were eager to get in where the fighting promised to be hottest and the danger most threatening.

All day long on May 30th we waited for those orders, and General Bundy reported that the division was ready. In the afternoon we received orders to be ready to leave at 6 o'clock on camions which would be provided. No word came from Division Headquarters, however, to indicate where we were going. We hoped and waited.

Six o'clock approached and no camions appeared. Then the orders were changed to 10 o'clock. Night fell, and still no camions. Indefinite orders came to be ready to leave at any time on short notice. The battalions were assembled and inspected and the men bivouacked in battalion groups.

All night they slept there in the open, on the ground. It was not until 4 o'clock on the morning of the 31st that the first camion arrived. They were big, powerful motor trucks, these camions, all French machines, with seats at the sides and with canvas covers like those of prairie schooners. The French had enough of them to move a quarter of a million troops. Many of them had Chinese drivers.

They came in convoys of fifty or so for each battalion, and they were quickly loaded. About thirty men were packed into each camion, each man with his rifle and sixty-pound pack. At 5.30 they started. The Marines were taken by battalions as they came, the first to go being a battalion of the Fifth under Lieutenant Colonel Wise.

There was a French officer in charge of each battalion. He rode in an automobile and took the battalion officers with him. I waited until the last squad of the Sixth had started, and then followed in my own car. For the entire division there was a steady stream of motor trucks pouring out from that region from 5.30 till nearly 10 A. M.

We were some seventy-five miles from our destination and many of the units made it a longer trip than that. On the whole the roads were good, but the journey had its exciting incidents. Most of those camions had been working for seventy-two hours at a stretch, carrying troops, and the drivers were worn out. Some of them fell asleep at their wheels and several ran off the road into the ditch.

As to our men, they were fresh and eager after their night on the hard ground. We must have seemed an extraordinary spectacle to the inhabitants of the country through which we passed, the interminable caravan of motor lorries filled with merry men in khaki, and the long train of artillery, machine guns, supply wagons, mules, and automobiles. They seemed to know what it meant, for they cheered us lustily on our way.

We skirted Paris, about nine miles to the south of us, and passed through pretty villages, in many of which the people were out in full force, waving small American flags and throwing flowers into the camions. It was more like an enormous bridal procession than a column of fighters going to face a terrible death.

The division started first for Meaux, and until we

arrived there we had no idea of whither we were bound or what we were to do. I arrived in Meaux about 8.30 that evening, after a hard all-day run, the troops having already passed through the town on their way to the front. I remained in Division Headquarters for half an hour, getting instructions, maps, etc.

Then followed a series of misadventures that tried my soul. From Meaux my first orders were to proceed north, but those orders were changed twice during the night. About 10 o'clock a French staff officer stopped my car and told me that the troops had been shunted off. I started in a new direction and was switched again to Montreuil-aux-Lions. I was a lost Colonel, hunting around in the dark for his command, and hunting with an anxiety that, in this crisis, approached panic.

There is no use in trying to conceal the fact that it was a sorry mix-up. The French were on the run, and the staff came pretty close to being up in the air. Orders were given and countermanded in the effort to get the reinforcements to the spot where they were most needed, while a dozen spots looked equally dangerous. It must have been a terrible night for those upon whose shoulders rested the responsibility of saving their beloved Paris.

After leaving Meaux I overtook a stream of our camions and met a number coming back. Sometimes there was a jam in the road that delayed the advance for ten minutes, due to some break-down of the overworked motors. Some of our troops were badly held up, or were lost in trying to find another way around. My regimental band didn't get to the front for two whole days.

I also began to meet sorry-looking little bands of refugees in the midst of all this traffic, wandering like lost souls in a chaos of confusion. I wondered, as I looked into their sad, resigned faces, whether they saw any hope or comfort in this long train of soldiers and guns. For the most part everything and everybody seemed to be hurrying away from the battle line except the Americans.

At Montreuil, about four miles back from the front, some of the troops left the camions and went into billets, but many of them got no sleep before daylight on June 1st, the very day we went into the line. And remember that the night before they had slept on the ground with the expectation of being called at any moment.

Our Marines rode on those camions from nineteen to thirty hours, according to their luck in reaching their destination. Some got lost and had to hike with their sixty-pound packs. When they arrived they were grey with dust and hollow-eyed with fatigue. They looked more like miners emerging from an all-night shift than like fresh troops ready to plunge into battle.

About midnight the first and luckiest battalion halted about seven kilometres back of where they were to go in. They expected orders to advance at once, but they got a little rest. There behind the lines, within sound of the booming guns, the men bivouacked, each with his poncho and one blanket, and waited for the day.

About noon on June 1st a battalion of the Fifth came trudging wearily in. They had been landed at the wrong place and had been obliged to march all the forenoon. Two battalions of the Sixth were delayed, Major Holcomb's battalion coming up in the afternoon just in time to be deployed into line from the trucks. Our supply train did not arrive till two days later.

Well, we all got there, but not much rest was allowed to the weary. A French staff officer had told me that we wouldn't be expected to go in until June 2nd, but General Harbord had determined to waste no time. If the need was urgent, delay might be fatal. And the Marines, he said, were always ready.

I think the French hesitated to trust us too far in this crisis. We were without tanks, gas shells, or flame projectors. We were untried in open warfare. But General Harbord begged to be allowed to tackle the job.

"Let us fight in our own way," said he, "and we'll stop them."

The situation was acute; there seemed to be no alternative. General Harbord was given free rein, and in that moment we passed out from our French tutelage and acted as an American army fighting side by side with our hard-pressed Allies. The Battle of Belleau Wood was fought by American troops, under American officers, supported by American guns, in a typically American manner. And the battle was won.

Orders came from General Harbord to move two battalions into line at once. I sent them up in the camions on the Metz-to-Paris road to within half a mile of the line of battle. From there they went in on foot. I went up with the camions and got there with the first of them. The Germans had some field guns—77's—trained on the road, but luckily they did not shell our trucks.

I say we sent them up in camions, but that is not wholly correct. Two battalions marched four miles from Montreuil to the line, but we managed to gather together about twenty-five lorries to carry most of the others.

It is easy enough to figure out how little genuine rest those men had had for over two days and nights, and how much fatiguing labour. And for two days more they had no food but their reserve rations of hardtack and bacon. (Each Marine carries reserve rations for two days in his pack—one pound of bread and three-fourths of a pound of bacon per day.) It came pretty close to hardship, but I heard no one complain.

Private John C. Geiger of Jasper, Fla., told about it later in the hospital. "The Dutchmen were about fifteen hundred yards away when we came on the scene," said he. "We got orders to dig in. We used the lids of our mess gear and bayonet for tools.

"Say, you'd be surprised to know just how much digging you can do under those circumstances.

Bullets and shrapnel came from everywhere. You'd work until it seemed you couldn't budge another inch, when a shell would hit right close and then you'd start digging with as much energy as if you had just begun."

The enemy artillery and machine gun fire annoyed Geiger, but the thing that made him cross was the irregularity of the meals, especially when an order came to move just as they were sitting down to the first warm meal in several days. "When you missed chow, then you missed something," said he, looking mournful at the recollection.

They say the German soldiers fight blindly, with only such knowledge of their objectives as is absolutely necessary to send them forward. We believe in giving our men thorough orientation and a realization of just what is expected of them and what they are up against. I showed the battalion commanders my map, indicating the points to be held, and through them passed on to the men all the information available. I hold that men like ours fight none the worse for knowing just what they are fighting for.

The men were told that the orders were to hold the line at all costs, for at first we were to assume a defensive position. Unquestionably they realized what that meant. They knew that there were few if any troops in their rear, for they had just come that way. They knew that only their thin, determined line lay between Paris and awful destruction, and in that knowledge they fought.

There was no distinct line where we went in—no trenches or prepared defences. We were merely ordered to take up a definite position in support of the French who were struggling in front with the advancing Germans. The latter were thrusting down columns wherever the resistance was weakest, forging ahead at the rate of six or seven miles a day, and the French line was not holding. Stragglers were coming through all the time, many of them at a loss as to the location of their units.

It was a tragedy, a heart-breaking, world-shaking tragedy, this defeat and demoralization of the heroic French troops who had fought so brilliantly for three years in defence of their native land. Pity swelled our hearts as we watched them stagger back to the rear, a bruised and broken remnant, with utter despair written upon their war-weary faces. To them the war was lost, life held no hope. We wanted to take them by the hand and say, "Brother, at last we have come." And when we took our places in the line of defence before Belleau Wood it was with the grim determination to avenge to the death the bitterness which had been shot into the hearts of those suffering men.

And oh, the peril to Paris and to the cause of liberty and justice that lay in that ebbing tide! If the world was staggered by the news of it, think what it must have meant to us who were there to witness it. Already we could hear the savage breakers snarling against the wreck-strewn reef that was our advance line. The storm was approaching, and it was borne in upon us that the war was lost if we did not hold.

Our first position can best be understood by consulting the diagram. The curving line which was assigned to our division ran from the Metz-to-Paris Road at La Thiolet in a generally northwesterly direction along the Bois des Clerembauts, through Triangle Farm, skirting the southern end of the Bois de Belleau, to the town of Lucy de Bocage; thence to Hill 142 and through Les Mares Farm to-

DIAGRAM 3

Showing the line from which the French fell back and the first position taken up by the Marines before Belleau Wood. Each square is one kilometre across.

ward the Bois de Veuilly. At the extreme left were the French and the 23rd Infantry. From Les Mares to Hill 142 the line was held by a battalion of the Fifth under Lieutenant Colonel Wise. From Hill 142 the First Battalion of the Sixth under Major Shearer took the line down past Lucy to a point just south of Belleau Wood. There it was joined by the Second Battalion of the Sixth—Holcomb's—which extended down to the Metz-to-Paris Road, where it was met by the Ninth Infantry. The Sixth Machine Gun Battalion was distributed along the line.

The Marines thus held a line extending from Les

Mares Farm, past Belleau Wood, to the road, a front
of seven kilometres in all. The Third Battalion of
the Sixth—Sibley's—was in support position in the
woods south of Lucy, about a mile and a half back
of the line, where it remained that night and the
next day. The other two battalions of the Fifth
were also in reserve.

As our men went into line there was a very light
artillery fire from the German guns, which seemed
to indicate a lack of information on the part of the
enemy as to the significance of the movement. It did
not bother us much. The men were ordered to dig
in and they made for themselves such shallow rifle
pits and shelter trenches as were necessary for protection in a temporary line.

There were three French regiments in front of the
Sixth at that time and one in front of the battalion
of the Fifth that went in. I went to Lucy, and there
I found a battalion of French troops and the Colonel
of the sector. He realized the desperate straits the
French troops were in and his mute appeal, as he
gazed questioningly into my eyes, was a prayer that
the Americans might show the stuff of men and hold
fast against the awful tide that threatened to engulf
all that life held dear to him.

On that first night two companies of Engineers,
which had been sent to us by General Bundy from Division Headquarters, reported to me. Their officers
found me in my temporary quarters in a corner of the
woods at 3 A. M. They were of great assistance to
us in preparing our positions, both then and later. In

the line the men made themselves as comfortable as they could for the night and feasted on bread and bacon.

The Ninth Regiment, as I have said, was given a position on our right at the Metz-to-Paris Road. On our left was a regiment of French troops. The 23rd Infantry arrived late, and so was sent in at the left of the French, though later they moved over.

It was in this line that we lay on the night of June 1st, waiting for the morrow.

CHAPTER VII

CARRYING ON

I ESTABLISHED my first Post of Command in a corner of the woods near Lucy-le-Bocage, but this soon proved to be too exposed a position as German shells began to burst in the neighbourhood, and on June 2nd I moved my P. C. over to La Voie du Chatel, a little village west of Lucy and south of Champillon. Here I established headquarters in an old stone house, and from here I had an excellent view of the battle ground. Later on, however, when the line was shortened, I moved again still farther south to the wooded cover of Mont Blanche, and Colonel Neville of the Fifth moved to my old P. C.

When Major Holcomb first went in he took quarters in an old stone farmhouse not far from his part of the line, but a shell hit that farmhouse early in the game and killed five men, and Holcomb took to the woods for greater security.

On June 2nd, after a night that could not have been entirely restful, our men awoke to the realization that the French were filtering through. The Germans kept up their steady push and the French continued to fall back. It became more and more clearly evident that we had come not a moment too soon and that we had been cast for a rôle at the

centre of a seething stage.   There could be no doubt
of the fact that the United States Marines must
build a dike against that onsweeping flood of destruction or nobody would.

All that day we waited for the crash which did
not come until late afternoon.   Fatigue and hunger
were forgotten in the excitement of the moment, and
when the crash came the Marines were ready.

The attack was launched against the French who
had remained in front of Wise's battalion of the
Fifth at Hill 165.   It started about 5 o'clock in the
afternoon and came from the north and northeast.
It was a beautiful, clear day, and from my post of
observation at La Voie du Chatel I could watch the
whole of it.

The Germans swept down an open slope in platoon
waves, across wide wheat fields bright with poppies
that gleamed like splashes of blood in the afternoon
sun.   The French met the attack and then fell
steadily back.   First I saw the French coming back
through the wheat, fighting as they came.   Then
the Germans, in two columns, steady as machines.
To me as a military man it was a beautiful sight.
I could not but admire the precision and steadiness
of those waves of men in grey with the sun glinting
on their helmets.   On they came, never wavering,
never faltering, apparently irresistible.

But they were not irresistible.   Back of the French
was a force they had not reckoned on, a force as
steady and confident as themselves.   It was that
battalion of the Fifth Marines on our left.

At the right moment the Americans opened up with a slashing barrage. Shrapnel, machine gun, and rifle fire was poured into those advancing lines. It was terrible in its effectiveness. The French told us that they had never seen such marksmanship practised in the heat of battle. If the German advance had looked beautiful to me, that metal curtain that our Marines rang down on the scene was even more so.

The German lines did not break; they were broken. The Boches fell by the scores there among the wheat and the poppies.

They hesitated, they halted, they withdrew a space. Then they came on again. They were brave men; we must grant them that. Three times they tried to reform and break through that barrage, but they had to stop at last. The United States Marines had stopped them. Thus repulsed with heavy losses they retired, but our fire was relentless; it followed them to their death. They broke and ran for cover, though their first line hung on till dark, north of Champillon.

Then, mercilessly, methodically, we shelled the woods where they had taken refuge. A French aviator who sailed overhead saw one entire battalion annihilated there, and signalled back "Bravo!" to our gunners.

It was a terrible slaughter; the mere thought of such wholesale killing is enough to curdle Christian blood. But we had whipped the Hun. We had turned that part of his advance into a rout. We had tasted his blood and we had not forgotten the blood of our own who had been slain. We had won our first fight there where fighting meant so much, and it would not have been human to refrain from cheering when it was over. And the men who had done it, that battalion of the Fifth Marines, were the ones who had walked all the way to Belleau Wood two days before, when their camions broke down.

Here is the story of that encounter as told by one of our Marines in a letter home:

"The Boches were coming with seven-league boots when General Harbord threw a line of Americans across the front and ordered us to hold.

"'Get the devils,' yelled Captain Blanchfield (now dead).

"A minute later the Boches tore out of the woods, a machine gun to every ten of them. A rain of good American lead from good American riflemen met them. We saw them stop. Surprised? Why, they never dreamed of anything like it. We kept pounding and they turned and raced back for the wood. The German drive got its first shock.

"We lay in the open, digging in with bayonets and firing while the Boche was frantically passing back word that a cog in the wheel had slipped. They still never dreamed of Americans, we later learned from prisoners."

This is the way one of our machine gunners, a Toledo boy, described his part in the action:

"I got your Dutchmen for you with a machine gun, lots of 'em, not over three hundred yards away, and one with a pistol for good luck. He bayoneted my bunkie and

he won't do it again. He's a good Fritz now. They
couldn't kill me, but it was almost as bad. I've still got
both my hands and legs, but my head is all to the bad
even yet.

"Up to this time we had been under some pretty severe barrages, but this time we must have gotten under
Fritz's skin because it started to rain shells of every
calibre from one-pounders to the big 'Sea Bags,' or nine-
inch howitzers.

"It lasted just an even hour and then Fritz came at
us with blood in his eye. I estimated them at about 500
and they were in fairly compact masses. We waited
until they got close, oh, very close. In fact, we let them
think they were going to have a lead pipe cinch.

"Oh, it was too easy; just like a bunch of cattle coming
to slaughter.

"I always thought it was rather a fearful thing to take
a human life, but I felt a savage thrill of joy and I could
hardly wait for the Germans to get close enough. And
they came arrogant, confident in their power, to within
300 yards.

"Curiously the infantry, which had been steady up to
this time, paused as though waiting for us of the 'devil's
snare drums' to take up the great work. And we did!
Rat-tat-tat-tat full into them, and low down, oh! But
it was good to jam down on the trigger, to feel her kick,
to look out ahead, hand on the controlling wheel, and see
the Heinies fall like wheat under the mower. They were
brave enough, but they didn't stand a chance. The poor
devils didn't know they were facing the Marines—
Americans.

"That hour paid in full all the weary hours of drill
and hike, all the nerve-racking minutes passed under
Fritz's barrage, and avenged the staring eyes and mangled

bodies of our dead buddies.   There weren't many of them
got back to tell the tale of the American's 'cowardice.'

"It was on the afternoon of this day that I got mine.
I had helped carry a wounded man back to the dressing
station and was coming back up the road.   I heard it (the
shell) whistle and knew it was going to hit close.   (You
can tell by the whistle when they are going to hit.)

"I jumped into a hole and the shell hit it at the same
time.   A blinding, deafening roar, and a sensation of
hurtling through space, and then oblivion—until several
days ago.   I have one faint recollection of bleeding terribly at the nose and ears, and the soft hands of an angel
working over me, and then darkness again.

"The Red Cross, especially those organizations near
the front, are beyond comparison.   How they must have
taken care of me and hundreds worse.   I haven't words
with which to express my praise.

"How do I feel?   Sometimes I'm all right and again
I'm not.   I have spells in which everything leaves me for
hours at a time and I can't tell for the life of me what I
did during that time.   And when I go in the sun I get
dizzy and bleed at the nose and my head feels like scram-
bled eggs most of the time."

On the night of June 2nd the French retreat became general.   They passed through to the rear in
large numbers, both stragglers and organized units,
and we suddenly realized that our line, which had
been placed here for support, had become, through
the fortunes of battle, the front.   The United States
Marines stood face to face with the oncoming hordes
of Attila.

Not for a moment did a sense of panic follow that

realization. Not a man thought of such a thing as joining the retreating French. There arose, rather, a sort of feeling of exultation, that now at last there was men's work to be done, the work of Marines in a tight place. All through the training at Quantico and before, all through the toilsome weeks in the trenches, they had been living for this chance, and now it had come. As to the officers, well, we had the whole history of the Corps behind us, and what a Marine has he holds; he kills or gets killed; he does not surrender; he does not retreat.

The retiring French made a gap in our line which we closed by putting in three reserve companies next to the battalion of the Fifth, so that the Sixth held a wide front of nearly seven kilometres, with one company in reserve. And we determined at all costs to hold that line.

There is no gain in mincing matters; the French were thoroughly demoralized. And they had good reason to be. They had been fighting interminably, pounded by guns, poisoned with gas, and borne back and broken by superior numbers. They were ordered to make a last stand, to counter-attack on the morning of June 3rd, but the units were disorganized; the officers simply couldn't get their men together. All that forenoon a distracted French officer stood near my Post of Command trying to stem the ebbing tide and to corral enough men to reorganize. That afternoon they did make a heroic though feeble attempt to counter-attack, but they were driven back, and fell in behind our lines.

During the 3rd there came a little relief in the form of motor trucks loaded with extra rations, but we had no way of cooking them. The men had to get along as best they could with bread, cold bacon, and "monkey" or tinned beef. Their only drinking water was in their canteens, and the source of supply was a mile or more away. In the midst of all this grim, tense seriousness there was something irresistibly ludicrous in the sight of our tireless runners hurrying back and forth all covered over with tinware, as they went for the precious water.

In the afternoon our mule-drawn supply train reached Montreuil with Major Manney of the Sixth and Major Puryear of the Fifth in command. They had realized the acuteness of the crisis and had accomplished the impossible. They had driven those mules fifty-five miles in twenty-two hours, without sleep or rest. They came, and with them came blessed Lizzie, back-firing and steaming, but ready to leap over the shell-torn roads to carry aid and comfort to the men at the front. The rolling kitchens were moved up to within two miles of the line, and from the 4th on we did our own cooking and every night sent at least one hot meal and hot coffee to the men.

It took about all night on June 3rd to get our lines well established and ready for the next onslaught. We pushed outposts into the smaller woods near Belleau and improved our defences and our gun positions. And that night the French liaison officers were withdrawn and the front line—that narrow but vital section of the Frontier of Liberty —was turned over to the United States Marines. Thenceforth we were to fight on our own.

Unquestionably the Germans were tremendously surprised by the unexpected resistance they had met. They couldn't have known who we were, for they had taken no steps to shell our lines and they took no prisoners who would reveal our identity. But they did know now that some sort of effective reinforcements had been brought up. They had been driving the French at will and now they were stopped.

As a matter of fact, the Germans had become too confident; perhaps Foch had counted on that. Relatively speaking, they were loafing on the job when we came up. It had all been so easy, and now they were only waiting to bring up more men and enough guns to start the final drive and administer the *coup de grace*.

They waited a day or two too long, for we were able to establish our lines without great hindrance, and on the 3rd American artillery had been brought up to support our division. Infantry action has accomplished wonders in this war on both sides, but however brilliant their performance, foot soldiers are not enough to check a big drive or carry through a big offensive. It was becoming more and more a war of artillery, and the Boche made his fatal mistake when he gave us a chance to bring up our guns.

Three regiments of artillery came to our support in this crisis—all Americans. The Twelfth and Fifteenth operated 75's; the Seventeenth was sup-

plied with heavies—French 155's. They took up
their positions the day they came in, the light guns
about a mile or a mile and a half back of the lines,
some of them near my Post of Command. The
heavies were about three miles back. All were
camouflaged, but the lighter guns were well within
the range of the enemy's observation and their
positions were frequently changed. As will be seen
later, these guns were unable to do fully effective
work at first, but in the end, after the Marines had
got the enemy on the run and had felt out all his
positions, they drove the last Germans from Belleau
Wood. To the Marines, in those last gruelling days,
their help meant everything.

By the 4th, the Germans seemed to have gained an
inkling of what was in front of them, for their shell
fire increased materially, and for two days the bombardment was terrific. There was the constant roar
of heavy guns, punctuated by the explosions of
bursting shells. They had evidently succeeded in
bringing up some of their 150's, and they appeared
to be preparing the ground for an advance.

During the 3rd and 4th our casualties from shell
fire numbered over 200—twenty dead and 195
wounded. The casualties were heaviest in the woods
at the rear where our reserves were located. Possibly
the Germans did not yet realize that we were actually
holding the front line. They shelled all the crossroads, to get our supplies and moving troops and to
cut our communications. They shelled Lucy heavily, then a battalion P. C. The shells fell so thickly in

the town that you could scoop up handfuls of shrapnel bullets in the streets—round pellets about the size of marbles. On the 4th, too, they began using gas, so that the men were obliged to fret away the hours in their stifling masks.

By this time our lines were pretty well consolidated and formed a long row of shallow rifle pits and shelter trenches where the men had dug themselves in. The men in reserve, warned by the shrapnel fire, had also dug in. I went down to inspect them on the 4th. Each man had dug a hole six feet long, two and a half feet wide, and three feet deep. Even the battalion commander had his hole. They looked shallow and open enough, but they did help; they offered good protection against flying shell splinters—against everything, in fact, except a direct hit. Under cover of darkness the men crept out to stretch their limbs, but they spent most of the daytime sleeping in their holes.

They were arranged in rows like graves in a Potter's Field or a soldiers' cemetery. The men, in fact, jocosely referred to them as their graves. When I saw them each was filled with the motionless form of a sleeping man. It was a gruesome sight.

We were not quite satisfied with the disposition of our forces, and on the night of the 4th we reformed our line, and the front held so thinly by the Marines was greatly shortened.

On the left, Wise's battalion of the Fifth was relieved by the French, who had now somewhat recovered and took over the line as far as Hill 142.

The First Battalion of the Sixth was also withdrawn
to support, and Major Berry's battalion of the Fifth
was sent in there to hold the line from Hill 142 to
Lucy, a shorter line than that held by the Sixth's

DIAGRAM 4

Showing the second position taken by the
American forces before Belleau wood on the
night of June 4th.

battalion. Holcomb
moved over with his
battalion of the Sixth,
until his left rested on
Lucy, joining Berry
there, and the 23rd
Infantry was brought
around to Holcomb's
new right at Triangle
Farm, where it held
the line from Triangle
to the road, making
contact with the
Ninth Infantry there.

The centre, therefore, was still held by Marines,
though on a much shorter front than before, there
being two of our battalions now in the line—Berry's
of the Fifth and Holcomb's of the Sixth—supported
on the left by the French and on the right by the
23rd Infantry. These new lines were successfully
consolidated and we faced the future with confidence
and a more effective formation.

To the north of our lines and to the west of Belleau
Wood the Germans still held too many strong points
for our comfort. The shell fire from Hill 165 was
particularly troublesome, and it was decided that an
attack was necessary to put these guns out of action.

About 3 o'clock on the morning of June 5th a joint attack was made by a French battalion and Berry's battalion of the Fifth. The enemy was taken by surprise and was driven back toward Torcy.

Many of his guns were put out of action and he was thrust back about a kilometre and a half to the north. I did not see that attack, and so I cannot describe it, but it was a brilliant action, and it resulted in our establishing a new line which the French held on the north, Berry's

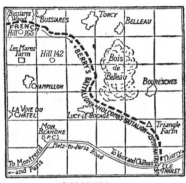

DIAGRAM 5

Showing the Allied line as advanced to the north on the morning of June 5th, after the successful Franco-American attack on Hill 165

men digging in along the western side of Belleau Wood.

It was on the 5th that, owing to the likelihood of early action, I moved my P. C. again, leaving Mont Blanche and returning to the neighbourhood of Lucy. By this move to an apparently more dangerous location it is probable that my life was saved, for a German shell reduced to a heap of ruins the room I had occupied at Blanche Farm very soon after I vacated it.

We now stood facing the dark, sullen mystery of Belleau Wood, Berry on the west and Holcomb on the south. It was a mystery, for we knew not what terrible destruction the Hun might be preparing for us within its baleful borders, nor at what moment it might be launched in all its fury against us. That the wood was strongly held we knew, and so we waited.

It was rolling country, with small woods scattered all about and farm land between. From many of the little hills a good view could be obtained of a considerable expanse of beautiful, pastoral landscape.

Of these woods Belleau was the largest, being about two kilometres from north to south and something over a kilometre from east to west. A kilometre is about three fifths of a mile. It was, therefore, not a large forest, but it loomed up before us like a heavy, menacing frown in the landscape. It was a typical piece of well kept French woodland, which the foresters had thinned and cared for so that the timber was of fairly uniform size and the underbrush fairly well cleaned out inside. At the edges there was some undergrowth and smaller trees and saplings. The timber was not large but grew very thickly. The trees were rather tall. I should say they would not average more than five or six inches in diameter, but they were set so closely that when our men got in they found they could see not more than fifteen or twenty feet through the wood, except where ax or shell fire had made small clearings. Belleau Wood stood on high, rocky ground and hid innumerable gullies and boulder heaps.

We were nearer to the woods on the south than on the west, and on both sides open wheat fields lay between our lines and the forest. From without it appeared almost impenetrable, and there were those open spaces to cross. Behind us lay the smaller woods where our own reserves were waiting.

The character of the terrain and the impossibility of gaining any information of the enemy's movements by direct observation added materially to the tenseness of the situation. It is hard to lie and wait for your antagonist to strike the first blow, but thus far we had received no orders save to act on the defensive and hold the line.

All through June 5th we waited, with nothing of moment occurring save increasing artillery fire on both sides. The sound of it was at times deafening. To this day I do not know why the Germans did not attempt a sortie—whether they felt so secure in their position that they could afford to wait for overwhelming reinforcements, or whether the resistance and then the offensive dash of the Fifth Marines had frightened them into caution.

As a matter of history, they never did come out, for on the following day the Marines went in.

CHAPTER VIII

"Give 'Em Hell, Boys!"

THE morning of June 6th found us holding the shortened line that I have just described, with Berry's battalion of the Fifth and Holcomb's of the Sixth in front and Sibley's of the Sixth in immediate support. That something was going on within those threatening woods we knew, for our intelligence men were not idle. Every day my regimental intelligence officer rendered a report of the enemy's movements to the Divisional Intelligence Department and also to me, and I reported in turn to Brigade Headquarters. The report on this morning was to the effect that the Germans were organizing in the woods and were consolidating their machine gun positions, so that a sortie in force seemed not unlikely.

As a matter of fact, we had been prepared for something of the sort for nearly two days. On the night of the 4th Lieutenant Eddy, the intelligence officer of the Sixth, with two men stole through the German lines and penetrated the enemy country almost as far as Torcy. They lay in a clover field near the road and watched the Germans filing past them. They listened to the talk and observed what was going into the woods.

It was a risky thing to do, but they brought back valuable information. This Lieutenant Eddy was a dare-devil, anyway, and loved nothing better than to stalk German sentries in Indian fashion and steal close to their lines. While we were in the trenches he did some remarkable work with the patrols. He was the son of a missionary, I believe, born and raised in Asia Minor, and was an American college graduate. How he came by his extraordinarily adventurous spirit, I don't know, but he certainly had it. The Marine service has always attracted men of that type.

As I say, we were looking for a sortie, but none came, and in the afternoon we were ordered to attack at 5 P. M. The Germans must be driven out of Belleau Wood.

There were sound strategic reasons for this remarkable order. In the first place, pressure had to be relieved northwest of Château-Thierry before that position could be made secure. Belleau Wood now formed a dangerous salient in our curving line, and to straighten that line from the advanced position at the northwest down to Triangle Farm, it was necessary to take in the town of Bouresches and at least a part of the wood.

In the second place, Belleau Wood was too strong a natural fortress to be allowed to remain in the hands of a powerful enemy on our immediate front. It was strongly garrisoned with infantry and machine gunners, and the big guns were coming up. For the Germans it formed a base of attack that threatened our whole line to the south.   So long as they held it a sudden thrust was possible at any time, and such a thrust might mean untold disaster, probably the quick advance on Paris.   For us it was an effective barricade.   The Allies could not advance with that thorn in their side.

Obviously, Belleau Wood had to be taken, and that right quickly, whether we were to act successfully on the defensive or on the offensive.   It would have been suicidal to wait for the German attack.   An assumption of the offensive was the only solution. And so it turned out that the United States Marines, who had been called up to support the French in defence, were ordered to attack, and to attack an enemy position of the strongest kind.   That we were expected to succeed speaks volumes for the confidence that we had won.

Belleau Wood is longer than it is wide, and the easiest way to take it was from west to east.   Otherwise we would have been plunging against the enemy's deepest strength.

Holcomb's battalion was ordered to hold the line, while Sibley's was to come up, pass through it, and make the attack on the southern section of the woods, starting in on the western side.   The objectives for the first attack mentioned in the orders were the eastern edge of the woods and Bouresches.   Berry's battalion was to attack from the west on Sibley's left.

The second prearranged objective was another section of the woods and a line over the high ground south of Torcy.   The French and the rest of the

Fifth were to push on toward the north, with Torcy and the rest of the woods as the ultimate objective. As will be seen, a part of these objectives were attained promptly and decisively, while others were delayed.

The orders to attack at 5 o'clock were written at Brigade Headquarters, about three kilometres in the rear, at 2 P. M. At 3.45 a copy was handed to me by Lieutenant Williams, General Harbord's aide, who came up by motorcycle.

I was supposed to direct Berry's movements, though he had also received the orders from his own Regimental Headquarters. I telephoned at once to Berry's P. C. at Lucy, but his battalion was beyond reach and he was himself in the woods in their rear, a mile away. It had been impossible, on account of the heavy shelling, to run a telephone out to him. I sent runners, but I was sure they couldn't reach him before the attack would have to be made.

I must confess that this situation caused me considerable anxiety. I don t know whose fault it was, but the communications were far from perfect. It looked as though we would have to attack without proper coöperation, and as a matter of fact, that is what we did. I was fully aware of the difficulties of the situation, especially for Berry. He had 400 yards of open wheat field to cross in the face of a galling fire, and I did not believe he could ever reach the woods. It looked as though Sibley's battalion would have to bear the brunt of the action.

No one knows how many Germans were in those

woods. I have seen the estimate placed at 1,000, but there were certainly more than that. It had been impossible to get patrols into the woods, but we knew they were full of machine guns and that the enemy had trench mortars there. We captured five of their minnenwerfers later. So far as we knew, there might have been any number of men in there, but we had to attack just the same, and with but a handful. Sibley and Berry had a thousand men each, but only half of these could be used for the first rush, and as Berry's position was problematical, it was Sibley's stupendous task to lead his 500 through the southern end of the wood clear to the eastern border if the attack was not to be a total failure. Even to a Marine it seemed hardly men enough.

The men knew in a general way what was expected of them and what they were up against, but I think only the officers realized the almost impossible task that lay before them. I knew, and the knowledge left me little comfort. But I had perfect confidence in the men; that never faltered. That they might break never once entered my head. They might be wiped out, I knew, but they would never break.

It was a clear, bright day. At that season of the year it did not get dark till about 8.30, so we had three hours of daylight ahead of us.

As soon as I received the orders I got Holcomb and Sibley together at the former's headquarters, some 500 yards back of the line. With map in hand, I explained the situation to them without trying to gloss over any of its difficulties and gave them their orders. I found them ready. As we stood there, Sibley's battalion was filing by into a ravine, getting into position. The two Majors passed on the oral orders to the company commanders.

With Captain Laspierre I went on to Lucy, and from there to a point where I could observe the action. Perhaps I exposed myself unduly, but I was anxious about Berry and it seemed necessary for me to get as near his command as possible and to keep an eye on the whole proceeding.

As I went through Lucy, I passed around the left of Sibley's men, now waiting in the shelter trenches, ready to go over the top. They were equipped for action. When Marines go into line they travel in heavy marching order, but when they go in to fight it is in light marching order, with no extra clothing or any blankets. They carry twenty-odd pounds then. They all had their rifles and ammunition, and some of the men were equipped with hand or rifle grenades. The machine guns were in position, both those of the machine gun company of the Sixth and those of two companies of the machine gun battalion attached to the brigade. They were just back of the front line. Each company had eight automatic rifles and eight in reserve; all were used.

The men seemed cool, in good spirits, and ready for the word to start. They were talking quietly among themselves. I spoke to several as I passed. Some one has asked me what I said, what final word of inspiration I gave those men about to face sudden death. I am no speech maker. If the truth must be told, I think what I said was, "Give 'em Hell, boys!" It was the sort of thing the Marine understands. And that is about what they did.

On my left I passed some of Berry's men, the right end of his battalion. They, too, seemed to be ready and waiting for the leash to be slipped.

Our artillery fired for half an hour, shelling the woods, but there was no artillery preparation in the proper sense of the term. They had no definite locations and were obliged to shell at random in a sort of hit-or-miss fire. It must have been largely miss. The German artillery, on the other hand, increased its fire as Sibley's men went into line.

Before us stood the frowning wood, with its splintered trunks and shell-shattered branches, and with the little jungle of undergrowth at the edge filled with threat and menace. It was a moment of foreboding fit to shake nerves of steel, like entering a dark room filled with assassins.

No orders as to the adjustment of rifle sights had been given, as the range was point blank. Watches had been synchronized and no further orders were given. As the hands touched the zero hour there was a single shout, and at exactly 5 o'clock the whole line leaped up simultaneously and started forward, Berry's 500 and Sibley's 500, with the others in support.

Instantly the beast in the wood bared his claws. The Boches were ready and let loose a sickening machine gun and rifle fire into the teeth of which

the Marines advanced. The German artillery in
the woods increased the fury of its fire, and the
big guns at Belleau and Torcy, a mile and a half
away, pounded our advancing lines.

On Berry's front there was the open wheat field,
400 yards or more wide—winter wheat, still green
but tall and headed out. Other cover there was none.
On Sibley's left there was open grass land perhaps
200 yards wide; his right was close to the woods.

Owing to the poor communications, the two battalions engaged in what were virtually independent
actions, and, as I had feared, Berry got the worst end
of it. He had to face that wide open space, swept
by machine gun fire, with a flanking fire from the
direction of Torcy.

My eyes were on what Sibley's men were doing,
and I only knew in a general way what was happen-
ing to the battalion of the Fifth. But Floyd Gibbons, the correspondent of the *Chicago Tribune*, was
with Berry and saw it all. He was, in fact, seriously
wounded himself, and has lost an eye as a result.
Gibbons says that the platoons started in good order
and advanced steadily into the field between clumps
of woods. It was flat country with no protection of
any sort except the bending wheat. The enemy
opened up at once and it seemed, he says, as if the
air were full of red-hot nails. The losses were
terrific. Men fell on every hand there in the open,
leaving great gaps in the line. Berry was wounded
in the arm, but pressed on with the blood running
down his sleeve.

Into a veritable hell of hissing bullets, into that death-dealing torrent, with heads bent as though facing a March gale, the shattered lines of Marines pushed on. The headed wheat bowed and waved in that metal cloud-burst like meadow grass in a summer breeze. The advancing lines wavered, and the voice of a Sergeant was heard above the uproar:

"Come on, you ―― ― ――! Do you want to live forever?"

The ripping fire grew hotter. The machine guns at the edge of the woods were now a bare hundred yards away, and the enemy gunners could scarcely miss their targets. It was more than flesh and blood could stand. Our men were forced to throw themselves flat on the ground or be annihilated, and there they remained in that terrible hail till darkness made it possible for them to withdraw to their original position.

Berry's men did not win that first encounter in the attack on Belleau Wood, but it was not their fault. Never did men advance more gallantly in the face of certain death; never did men deserve greater honour for valour.

Sibley, meanwhile, was having better luck. I watched his men go in and it was one of the most beautiful sights I have ever witnessed. The battalion pivoted on its right, the left sweeping across the open ground in four waves, as steadily and correctly as though on parade. There were two companies of them, deployed in four skirmish lines, the

men placed five yards apart and the waves fifteen
to twenty yards behind each other.

I say they went in as if on parade, and that is
literally true.   There was no yell and wild rush, but
a deliberate forward march, with the lines at right
dress.   They walked at the regulation pace, because
a man is of little use in a hand-to-hand bayonet
struggle after a hundred yards dash.   My hands
were clenched and all my muscles taut as I watched
that cool, intrepid, masterful defiance of the German
spite.   And still there was no sign of wavering or
breaking.

Oh, it took courage and steady nerves to do that in
the face of the enemy's machine gun fire.   Men fell
there in the open, but the advance kept steadily on
to the woods.   It was then that discipline and
training counted.   Their minds were concentrated
not on the enemy's fire but on the thing they had
to do and the necessity for doing it right.   They
were listening for orders and obeying them.   In this
frame of mind the soldier can perhaps walk with even
more coolness and determination than he can run.
In any case it was an admirable exhibition of military
precision and it gladdened their Colonel's heart.

The Marines have a war cry that they can use to
advantage when there is need of it.   It is a blood-
curdling yell calculated to carry terror to the heart
of the waiting Hun.   I am told that there were wild
yells in the woods that night, when the Marines
charged the machine gun nests, but there was no
yelling when they went in.   Some one has reported

that they advanced on those woods crying, "Remember the *Lusitania!*" If they did so, I failed to hear it. Somehow that doesn't sound like the sort of thing the Marine says under the conditions. So far as I could observe not a sound was uttered throughout the length of those four lines. The men were saving their breath for what was to follow.

I am afraid I have given but a poor picture of that splendid advance. There was nothing dashing about it like a cavalry charge, but it was one of the finest things I have ever seen men do. They were men who had never before been called upon to attack a strongly held enemy position. Before them were the dense woods effectively sheltering armed and highly trained opponents of unknown strength. Within its depths the machine guns snarled and rattled and spat forth a leaden death. It was like some mythical monster belching smoke and fire from its lair. And straight against it marched the United States Marines, with heads up and the light of battle in their eyes.

Well, they made it. They reached the woods without breaking. They had the advantage of slightly better cover than Berry's men and the defensive positions at the lower end of the woods had not been so well organized by the Germans as those on the western side. The first wave reached the low growth at the edge of the woods and plunged in. Then the second wave followed, and the third and the fourth, and disappeared from view.

Some months later Private W. H. Smith, recovering from his wounds in the Naval Hospital in Brooklyn, told the story of that charge:

"There wasn't a bit of hesitation from any man. All went forward in an even line. You had no heart for fear at all. Fight—fight and get the Germans was your only thought. Personal danger didn't concern you in the least and you didn't care.

"There were about sixty of us who got ahead of the rest of the company. We just couldn't stop despite the orders of our leaders. We reached the edge of the small wooded area and there encountered some of the Hun infantry.

"Then it became a matter of shooting at mere human targets. We fixed our rifle sights at 300 yards and aiming through the peep kept picking off the Germans. And a man went down at nearly every shot.

"But the Germans soon detected us and we became the objects of their heavy fire. We received emphatic orders at this time to come back but made the half mile through the woods, hardly losing a man on the way."

I had no field telephone and felt obliged to see what was going on. I took my stand on a little rise of ground protected by a low line of bushes about 300 yards from the woods. It was near a road where Holcomb's left had been in contact with Berry's right. The shelter trenches did not cross the road. From this point of vantage I watched the advance through my glasses.

Bullets rained all around me, the machine gun crews near me forming a target for the Germans.

There was a great racket of rifle and machine gun fire and bursting shrapnel and high explosives, like the continuous roll of some demoniacal drum, with the bass note of the heavy guns that were shelling Lucy.

I saw a number of our brave lads fall in that advance. The German machine gunners aimed low to sweep the ground, catching most of the men in the legs. And those who fell lay right in the line of fire and many of them were killed there on the ground. Those who were able to stand and keep going had the best chance. Some of them went through the whole fight with leg wounds received druing the first ten minutes.

I am able to tell something of what went on in the woods that night, but my own participation in the conflict ended abruptly right there, and before continuing the narrative I may as well give a brief account of what happened to me.

Just about the time Sibley's men struck the woods a sniper's bullet hit me in the chest. It felt exactly as though some one had struck me heavily with a sledge. It swung me clear around and toppled me over on the ground. When I tried to get up I found that my right side was paralysed.

Beside me stood Captain Tribot-Laspierre, that splendid fellow who stuck to me through thick and thin. He had been begging me to get back to a safer place, but I was obstinate and he never once thought of leaving me. When I fell he came out of his cover and rushed to my side. He is a little man and I am not, but he dragged me head first back to the shelter trench some twenty or twenty-five feet away. My life has been spared and I owe much to that Frenchman.

I have heard of men getting wounded who said that it felt like a red-hot iron being jammed through them before the world turned black. None of these things happened to me. I suffered but little pain and I never for a moment lost consciousness. Nor did any thought of death occur to me, though I knew I had been hit in a vital spot. I was merely annoyed at my inability to move and carry on.

The bullet went clean through my right lung, in at the front and out at the back, drilling a hole straight through me. I am inclined to think that it was fired by a sniper in the trees at some distance to the left, who was trying to pot our machine gunners. I believe it was a chance shot and not the result of good marksmanship, for the bullet must have come some 600 yards.

Experts have made a study of the action of rifle bullets, and have discovered that a bullet fired at short range—less than 500 or 600 yards—twists in such a manner that when it strikes an obstacle it wabbles. If my bullet had been shot from near at hand it would have torn a piece out of my back as big as my fist. On the other hand, a spent bullet is already wabbling, and would have made a big hole in the front of my chest and perhaps would not have gone clear through. That is why I believe that my bullet came from a sniper about 600 yards away, and I am thankful that it did.

Captain Laspierre laid me down in the bottom of a three-foot trench and there I remained for an hour and a half. He opened my coat and shirt, but there was little he could do. Most of the bleeding was internal.

My runners were near at hand, and I had the Captain send a message by one of them to Lucy, whence the news of my wound could be telephoned back to the Post of Command, where Lieutenant Colonel Lee and my adjutant, Major Evans, were located. Lee jumped for the automobile and drove to Lucy; from there he came on foot to where I was' and I turned over the command of the regiment to him.

In about three quarters of an hour Dr. Farwell, the regimental surgeon, came from Lucy and administered first aid treatment. These trips all had to be made under heavy fire.

As I lay there before turning the orders of the day over to Lee, I was chiefly conscious of my anxiety over the outcome of the battle. My mind was as active as ever, and it was torture to lie there and not be able to see or do anything. I received reports from Sibley by runners, telling of his progress, and these I read to Lee when he came.

Dr. Farwell brought stretcher bearers with him, but I was kept there in the trench for a while because of the heavy artillery fire. Gas shells began to burst near us, and they put my gas mask on me. I never knew before how uncomfortable one of those things could be. It is hard enough for a man to breathe with a lung full of blood without having one of those smothering masks clapped over his face.

Fortunately, my interest was so firmly fixed on the fortunes of battle that I had but little time to indulge in any feeling of discomfort. I heard the sound of the firing gradually recede, and knew that Sibley's men were advancing. Then it came nearer on the left, and I knew that Berry's outfit was being beaten back. It was not an ideal way to observe an action, and my anxiety would have been almost unbearable if it had not been for one or two reassuring messages from Sibley. That grand old man was as hopeful as if the whole American army had been at his back.

After a while the artillery fire let up a little, though it was still on when they carried me back to Lucy. They cut off my mask and hauled me out of the ditch and bundled me on to the stretcher. Four men raised me to their shoulders and away we went. Carrying a 215-pound man on a stretcher over rough country under fire is no joke, but they got me to Lucy.

Meanwhile Sergeant Sidney Colford had got an ambulance at Lucy and I was rushed to the forward hospital and shot full of anti-tetanus serum. Then on to Meaux and finally to Paris, where I arrived at 4 A. M. the next day—June 7th—after being eight hours in the ambulance. I was placed in Hospital No. 2—Dr. Blake's—where they drew quarts of blood from my pleural cavity. It is a wonder that I came through it, but there were no serious complications and the wound began to heal. I remained in the hospital until July 22, when I was discharged and came home on leave.

So much for my personal experience. Meanwhile the battle for Belleau Wood was going on, and I received detailed reports of it. How it went with the boys after I fell remains now to be told.

CHAPTER IX

In Belleau Wood and Bouresches

MAJOR Burton William Sibley is one of the most picturesque characters in the Marine Corps. He is a short, swarthy man, wiry and of great endurance. He is one of those men whose looks are no indication of their age; he might be anywhere from thirty-five to fifty. I fancy that is why he is affectionately known as "the old man." As a matter of fact he was born in Vermont on March 28, 1877, and was appointed a Second Lieutenant of Marines on July 23, 1900. Thus far he seems to have borne a charmed life and I hope his luck will not desert him.

Sibley is particularly thorough in everything he does and has never been known to get rattled. His men love him and would follow him anywhere. He is as active as a boy, and it was he who, on foot and fighting as desperately as any of them, personally led those two companies of Marines into the death-haunted labyrinth of Belleau Wood. They followed him as warriors of old followed their chieftain, and he pulled them through and won the first stage of the battle that was to put the strength of our brigade to the acid test. Staunch veteran of Marines that he is, he deserves all the praise that can be heaped upon him for that night's work.

The minute they got into the woods our boys found themselves in a perfect hornets' next of machine gunners, grenadiers, and riflemen. No one could have realized how strong the enemy's position there was, or I do not believe that we would have been ordered in without more adequate artillery preparation. There were machine gun nests everywhere—on every hillock and small plateau, in every ravine and pocket, amid heaps of rocks, behind piles of cut timber, and even in the trees, and every gun was trained upon the advancing Marines and spitting hot death into them.

These German guns in the wood were well placed to cover all zones with both lateral and plunging fire. No spot was safe from their spray of bullets. Quick action was essential, or our force would have been wiped out. But the Marines never faltered. They attacked those nests with rifles, automatics, grenades, and bayonets. In small groups, even singly, they charged the machine gun crews and their infantry supports with wildcat ferocity, fighting like fiends till the Huns were dead or threw up their hands and bleated "Kamerad." Then they rushed on to the next one.

The most effective method was to run to the rear of each gun in turn and overpower the crew. But each flanking position was covered by another gun which had to be taken immediately. It was a furious dash from nest to nest, with no time to stop for

breath. In the thick of the mêlée the wild yells of
the Marines were mingled with the constant
crackle of rifle fire like bunches of fire crackers
exploding.

Through the smoke of battle that drifted like fog
among the tree trunks, Sibley kept to his course
across the southern section of the wood. His difficulties must have seemed well-nigh insuperable, for
his men were exposed to a constant flanking fire on
their left, while they were obliged to keep their eyes
to the front and take the machine guns from the
flank or rear. But take them they did, one after
another, and though many a brave man fell there in
the wood, they pushed steadily on across.

There was dense brush in spots, where men got lost
and found themselves isolated and cut off from their
squads. The wounded dragged themselves to thickets
and depressions—any place where they could hide
from those prying bullets and wait till there was time
for some one to carry them out. They were short of
water and the suffering of many of them was intense,
but they urged their comrades to leave them and
press on.

An hour passed; two hours, the Marines still fighting with the savage intensity of catamounts. "All
the time," said Private Frank Damron afterward,
"the fighting consisted in running from one shell
hole to another. Shove your bayonet at a Hun and
he will give up. I myself had very little 'sticking' to do. You could generally get them with a
rifle bullet first." "Our men," added Corporal John

Miles, "went after them with fixed bayonets, and drove them as a fellow drives a flock of chickens."

The action was all in the hands of the platoon officers. Success or failure rested on their shoulders. It is not the general who wins such a battle as that, but the captain, the sergeant, the private.

It had been called an exaggerated riot, that desperate conflict in the wood. It was hand-to-hand fighting from the first, and those Germans, hating cold steel as they do, soon learned what American muscle and determination are like. From tree to tree fought our Marines, from rock to rock, like the wild Indians of their native land. It is the sort of fighting the Marine has always gloried in. And in that fighting they beat the Germans on two points—initiative and daring, and accuracy of rifle fire. They picked the German gunners out of the trees like squirrels, and in the innumerable fierce onslaughts that took place at the machine gun nests the Marines always struck the first blow and it was usually a knock-out. It was a wild, tempestuous, rough-and-tumble scrap, with no quarter asked or given. Rifles grew hot from constant firing and bayonets reeked with German gore. It was man to man, there in the dark recesses of the woods, with no gallery to cheer the gladiators, and it was the best man that won.

The thick woods made the fighting a matter of constant ambuscades and nerve-racking surprises, but the Marines tore on. With Sibley at their head nothing could stop them. Machine gun nests whose crews held out formed little islands in the welter about which the Marine flood swept, eventually to engulf them. Some of the Germans turned and fled, abandoning their guns; others waited till caught in the rear and then threw up their hands and surrendered; some waited in huddled groups in the ravines till the gleaming-eyed devil dogs should leap upon them; some stuck to their guns till an American bullet or an American bayonet laid them low. One by one the guns were silenced or were turned in the opposite direction.

They started in at 5 o'clock. At 6.45 the report was sent to headquarters that the machine gun fire at the lower end of the woods had been practically silenced. At 7.30 German prisoners began to come in.

Night fell with the fighting still going on and only the flash of shooting to see by. But at 9 o'clock word came from Sibley by runner that he had got through and had attained the first objective, the eastern edge of the wood. In four hours he and his men had passed clear through the lower quarter of Belleau Wood, traversing nearly a mile, and had cleaned things up as they went. And only 500 of them started; I hesitate to mention the number that finished.

At 10 o'clock reinforcements were sent in with orders to consolidate the position. Two companies of Engineers were reported at Lucy and they were ordered in to help. Their assistance was invaluable, for though there was still heavy fighting for the

Marines that night, the Engineers started in at once and by morning had the position reasonably secured. Orders to stop further advance were sent out at the same time.

The men who went through that Turkish bath of fire and steel are the best judges of what it was like. This is the way the story was told by Private W. H. Smith of Winston-Salem, N. C., after he had been invalided home:

"German machine guns were everywhere. In the trees and in small ground holes. And camouflaged at other places so that they couldn't be spotted.

"We stayed for the most part in one-man pits that had been dug and which gave us just a little protection.

"We saw one German a short distance before us, who had two dead ones lying across him. He was in a sitting posture and was shouting 'Kamerad, Kamerad.' We soon learned the reason. He was serving as a lure and wanted a group of Marines to come to his rescue so that the kind-hearted Americans would be in direct line of fire from machine guns that were in readiness.

"Now isn't that a dirty trick? Say, it made me sore. Before I knew what I was doing and before I realized that every one was shouting at me to stay back I bobbed up out of my hole and with bayonet ready beat it out and got that Kamerad bird. It seemed but a minute or so before I was back. But, believe me, there were some bullets whizzing around. They came so close at times I could almost feel their touch. My pack was shot up pretty much but they didn't get me.

"After that I thought I was bullet proof, and didn't care a damn for all the Germans and their machine guns.

"Soon we charged forward again. I saw one Dutch-man stick his head out of a hole and then duck. I ran to the hole. The next time his head came up it was good-night Fritz.

"We were running along when a German pops up right up from the weeds on the roadside and shot at a Sergeant with me. The bullet got the Sergeant in the right wrist. I got the German before he dropped back into the weeds.

"Every blamed tree must have had a machine gunner. As soon as we spied them we'd drop down and pick them off with our rifles. Potting the Germans became great sport. Even the officers would seize rifles from wounded Marines and go to it.

"On the second day of our advance my Captain and two others besides myself were lying prone and cracking away at 'em. I was second in line. Before I knew what had happened a machine gun got me in the right arm just at the elbow. Five shots hit right in succession. The elbow was torn into shreds but the hits didn't hurt. It seemed just like getting five little stings of electricity.

"The Captain ordered two men to help me back. I said I could make it alone. I picked up the part of the arm that was hanging loose and walked.

"It was a two-mile hike to the dressing station. I got nearly to it when everything began to go black and wobbly. I guess it was loss of blood. But I played in luck, for some stretcher bearers were right near when I went down."

In a letter home Private Edward Cary of St. Louis thus described that night of blood and battle:

"We were called from a little town somewhere in the vicinity of the Marne, where we were resting, up to the front, where the Germans were coming too strong for the French, and when we hit the line the 'Froggies' were all in and retreating. The Marines went into the action, stopped them and drove them back over a mile. How's that?

"We did not go into action until the 6th, but were held in reserve in woods made a living hell by shell fire. I have seen boys killed and blown to pieces by high explosive shells right beside me. It was trying at first. A comrade was wounded alongside of me and one killed. The same shell got the both of them.

"The day after this we made an attack. Whooey! I never knew there were so many machine-gun bullets and high explosives in the world. Two men, one on either side of me, were killed by machine-gun fire, and in the fracas I lost the company but hooked up with another one. A Lieutenant, eight other men and myself took seventeen prisoners, three machine guns, and other equipment. I had to shoot at two of them, and they fell, and, as we found them afterwards dead, I have two notches to my credit.

"When we came up to the Germans they threw down their arms and called 'Kamerad! Mercy!' They are yellow as ochre and will not fight like men. As long as they are away from you they will fight, and fight damn dirty, but corner them and they quit—I could lick a squad of them with a soup ladle.

"Some of the boys took souvenirs, but not for me. Everything they own is tainted with innocent blood and they are too damn mean and too foul to touch. The only things that I have are three buttons that a young 16-year-old Prussian gave to me voluntarily.

"Well, we gave them hell that night when they attempted a counter-attack, and then we were relieved to go into reserve and reorganize. I wasn't the least bit scared in battle."

During the night the fighting raged for five hours or more with gradually diminishing fury, and those men who were able to snatch a few minutes' sleep in a shelter trench or rifle pit were the lucky ones.

Meanwhile an equally important and successful action against odds had been taking place at Bouresches, the town just east of the woods at its lower end. It was necessary to eject the Germans from this position for the same reasons that made it essential to drive them from Belleau Wood.

Shortly after the attack on Belleau Wood had been launched, the 96th Company of Holcomb's battalion and one of Sibley's reserve companies were ordered to take the town, and two platoons started, one from each company. There was a short bombardment, and then the Marines advanced in four waves just as the others had done in going into the wood—twelve men in each wave, five yards apart, and twenty yards between the waves. The first and third waves were supplied with automatics and grenades, the second and fourth with rifles. They advanced across a little valley and a wheat field, in the face of a sharp fire from three-inch and machine guns.

The original plan was to have the battalion of Sibley's company go into Bouresches, while Holcomb's undertook to straighten the line from there to Triangle Farm, but through some misunderstanding of the orders, Holcomb's men got to Bouresches first and went in.

Half of this little force was under Captain Duncan and the other half under Lieutenant Robertson. The enemy's fire, as they neared the town, was frightful, and more men fell than kept going. Duncan was shot down while coolly advancing with his pipe in his mouth. Robertson, who, by the way, was afterward shot through the neck near Soissons, led the remnant on and entered the town.

There were probably 300 to 400 Germans in that town and the place bristled with machine guns. There were guns at the street corners, behind barricades, and even on the housetops, but the Marines kept on. They attacked those machine guns with rifle, bayonet, and grenade in their bitter struggle for a foothold. They were outnumbered when they started, and one by one they were put out of the fighting. But they kept going, taking gun after gun, until the Germans, for all their numbers and advantage of position, began to fall back. And Lieutenant Robertson took Bouresches with twenty men!

He sent back word at 9.45 that he had got in and asked for reinforcements, but he did not wait for them. Those twenty men started in to clean up that town in the approved Marine fashion, and he was well on his way when Captain Zane's company of Holcomb's battalion arrived to support him. Then Engineers were sent in to help consolidate the position.

But the town was not yet fully won. The Germans began displaying counter-activity, and the

Marines sent back word that they were running short of ammunition.   Lieutenant William B. Moore, the Princeton athlete, and Sergeant Major John Quick (of whom more anon) volunteered to take in a truck load.   With a small crew chosen from fifty who wanted to go, they started with their precious, perilous freight, over a torn road under a terrific fire. The whole way was brilliantly lighted by enemy flares and the solitary truck offered a shining mark to the German gunners.   It rolled and careened fearfully over the gullies and craters, shells shrieked and whistled over their heads and burst on every hand, and as they neared the town they drove straight into the fire of the spouting machine guns.   But John Quick bears a charmed life and they got through unscathed.

That ammunition truck saved the day at Bouresches, for after it got in, Zane's men proceeded to clean up the town.   At 11 o'clock that night the report was sent in to headquarters to the effect that the Germans had been driven out of Boursesches. At 2.30 A. M. they made an attempt to get in again, but the counter-attack was smothered by our machine gun fire.

The next day, with the help of the Engineers, our position in the town was made secure.   Later the garrison was reinforced by replacement men under Quick.   Fighting continued through the 8th, but all counter-attacks were repulsed and the town remained in our hands.   Contact was established with Sibley's men in Belleau Wood and Holcomb

straightened and consolidated the line from Bouresches to Triangle Farm.

Through all this fighting our men were obliged to
get along without direct telephone connection with
headquarters, and our runners were depended upon
to carry out the reports and the requests for assistance. All that night they plied their hazardous
trade, dashing through machine gun and shell fire
and keeping open the lines of communication. They
were specially selected men, attached to headquarters, and their work should not be allowed to
pass unnoticed.

I have spoken of some of the officers who were
responsible for the success of our undertaking, but
I have neglected to mention Wendell Neville, the
Colonel of the Fifth. He was a classmate of mine
at Annapolis and we entered the Corps together.
He was with the Marines at Guantanamo and was
brevetted Captain there for his excellent work. He
served with Waller in China at the time of the Boxer
uprising and at Vera Cruz. After I was wounded
and Lee took over the command of the Sixth, Neville
went in with the Fifth in the subsequent fighting in
Belleau Wood. He is now a Brigadier General and
had command of the brigade at Soissons in July.

And I must speak of Major Evans. He had
retired from the service but rejoined at the outbreak
of war. He joined the Sixth Regiment when it
was organized and with the able assistance of John
Quick he whipped that regiment into shape at
Quantico. I couldn't have had a better man. He

is a jolly fellow, always in good spirits, and possesses
that sort of magnetic, dynamic personality that
keeps things moving. He is a man of intellect, too,
and altogether just the sort to succeed with our college
boys.

In France he served as my adjutant. He did not
get into the fighting in Belleau Wood and Bouresches
because he remained at the Post of Command,
where he received all the reports and orders and kept
his fingers constantly on the keys of the situation.
He backed up Sibley and Holcomb in their arduous
undertakings; his was the brain behind the fight.

A long letter from Major Evans, written from the
front to our Commandant, Major General George
Barnett, I have thought best to offer in full in the
appendix of this volume, since it gives a graphic
account of the entire action at Belleau Wood as
viewed by the man at the end of the wires in the
Post of Command. I will, however, insert at this
point a shorter letter from Major Evans to Mrs.
Charles A. Childs of New York, the donor of our
regimental colours, because it speaks entertainingly
of our old friend Lizzie who turned up again at
Bouresches.

"As a result of the splendid work of the Marine Brigade, notably between June 6th and 10th, when our regiment did its share in the capture of Bouresches and
part of the Bois de Belleau, we have learned that the
brigade is to be cited by the French army and that the
regimental colours will have the *Croix de Guerre* and the
palm. It is a wonderful honour, the highest that any

regiment has won over here so far, and I know how much you will be pleased and how proud you will be. When it does take place I will send you a photograph, as many as I can, if I have to face a firing squad to get them to you. We also hear that our Colonel, who was wounded in the first half hour of the first fight, is to be made a Chevalier of the Legion of Honour.

"And the Ford which Mrs. Pearce gave us will go down in Marine Corps history at any rate.

"Elizabeth Ford, as the regiment knows her, has had a unique career. Not only in Quantico, where I drove her, but in Bordeaux and later up in our training area, she carried everything from sick men to hard tack. Then we had two months in the trenches near Verdun and at the end it seemed as though she would have to go to the scrap heap. Her top was entirely gone and we made a mail wagon of her. In some way the men, who have an affection for her that you can hardly comprehend, patched her together and we brought her down to our first billets. A week later we had to go to another area, forty kilometres north of Paris, and in the long trip the Elizabeth Ford sailed along without mishap and was the talk of the division.

"Then we came up here and she rose to the heights of her service and her record. The night we took Bouresches with twenty-odd men, and news came through that others had filtered in and the town was ours, we shot out a truck load of ammunition over the road. The road was under heavy shell and machine gun fire. Later in the night we sent the Ford out with rations. For the next five days she made that trip night and day, and for one period ran almost every hour for thirty-six hours. She not only carried ammunition out to the men who were less than 200 yards from the Boche, but rations and pyrotechnics;

and then to the battalion on the left of the road, in those evil Belleau Woods, she carried the same, and water, which was scarce there. For these trips she had to stop on the road and the stores were then carried by hand into a ravine. I saw her just after her first trip and counted twelve holes made by machine gun bullets and shrapnel.

"At one time the driver, Private Fleitz, and his two understudies, Haller and Bonneville, had to stop to make minor repairs, and another time, when they had a blowout, how she and the men escaped being annihilated is a mystery. The last time I saw her she was resting against a stone wall in the little square of Lucy-le-Bocage, a shell wrecked town, and she was the most battered object in the town. One tire had been shot off, another wheel hit, her radiator smashed, and there were not less than forty hits on her. We are trying every possible way to find new parts and make a new Ford of her. She is our Joan of Arc and if it takes six old cars to make her run again we'll get those six and rob them."

As night deepened and hostilities diminished in Belleau Wood and Bouresches, the first stage of the battle ended, with our line extended some distance to the north, taking in nearly a third of the wood and the town of Bouresches, and running from there straight down to Triangle Farm. All night the indefatigable Engineers laboured to make good our position while the fighters snatched such rest as they could, and the dawn of June 7th found them ready for another attack on the monster in the forest.

CHAPTER X

Pushing Through

THE backbone of the German resistance was broken on the night of June 6th when Sibley went through Belleau Wood and Robertson walked into Bouresches, but there still remained much to be done. We held the town and the lower edge of the wood, but it was at best but a precarious foothold. The enemy remained in force to the north of the town, his machine guns were still thick in the greater part of the wood, and his big guns still thundered from back of Torcy. He was daunted by our first rush, but he came back. It took the Marines many days to finish the job, but finish it they did.

On June 7th fighting recommenced with a more intense fury, and our losses on that day were even heavier than on the 6th. We launched a series of battalion attacks against the forces in the wood, besides the constant fighting for local positions and the repulsing of counter-attacks. On that day Sibley's men resumed their rushing of machine gun nests and their strenuous hand-to-hand fighting.

At peep of day they were up and at 'em again as though fresh from their billets. It was now a matter of thrusting the whole line northward through the wood, and into its darksome maw they plunged, straight into its Dantean horrors. There was no respite. The enemy machine gun fire became more deadly after they had penetrated to some little distance, but they had to keep going. When they could they dug little rifle pits for themselves with the small trench tool carried in the kit, as a slight shelter against that withering fire. When fatigue became greater than could be borne, men curled up in shell holes or crevices in the rocks, or in the shallow trenches they dug, hoping for a brief respite, only to be roused by the uproar of a new conflict or the nearby bursting of a shell. Occasionally gas was poured into the wood, and that meant fighting in masks. None but the finest type of soldier could have stood up to all this and continue to make progress. They took those machine gun nests one after another, and in some cases were able to turn them on the Germans.

Our artillery was at a disadvantage in not knowing just how far our men had penetrated, but gradually, with more complete information, our shell fire improved. The guns coöperated when they could, eventually hurling more than 5,000 high explosive and gas shells into the woods and clearing the heights.

Fighting on in those treacherous woods, subject to flanking fire and in constant danger of ambush, the Marines continued to advance, regardless of fatigue and losses, until they held another quarter of a mile of the woods and the advance was halted. The new position was consolidated with the help of the Engineers and food and ammunition were sent in.

Lizzie did heroic work on that day. A few light guns were got in to Sibley.

As a result of the fighting of June 7th all along the line, the Americans advanced their position over a six-mile front.

On the 8th and 9th, Sibley's men continued to rush those machine gun nests and to make further progress in the wood. It seemed as if nothing could tire them out or force them back. Meanwhile, Berry, who had been wounded, was relieved. Lieutenant Colonel Wise, in command of his battalion of the Fifth, went in to support Sibley.

Our casualties were terrible; I will not attempt to give the figures. Our men were engaging in a sort of fighting that means heavy losses with the best of luck, but that did not check them. Their comrades fell, but they pressed on, and behind them they left dead Huns piled three deep about those captured nests.

To the men in the woods, fighting most of the time, snatching sleep when they could, the succession of night and day was hardly noticeable and there were few who could have told how long they had been fighting. Thus wrote Private George Budde of the Fifth to his parents:

"I was always glad when the various positions we held in the woods had a few holes strewn around into which we could crawl when necessary, but there were days in the first woods we went to especially, when M. and myself, he being of the same mind, lay under the stars with nothing but a blanket, while the others had gone from four to six feet under ground, which was not as foolish as it sounds, as the shells were really going over us, and besides there was a perfectly splendid ditch along the side of the road. I really did start to dig, but it just naturally tired me all to little bits and I quit with nothing to show for it but some elegant blisters. It seems really unbelievable, but there were hours at a time at that place and others when we would lie *perdu*, while a steady stream of missiles would be going sweetly over our heads, just a continuous humming whir-r-r that can't be described. Most of the big ones do give notice of their approach most politely, and one generally has time to duck or take cover."

On June 8th Major Evans jotted down a laconic memorandum to the effect that Holcomb had asked for both chaplains. That meant the hurried burial of our dead.

And right here let me put in a good word for those chaplains. Theirs is no easy berth, and they do not always receive the honour that is their due. The Marine chaplains, like the members of the Medical Corps, are furnished by the Navy. They are busy men. Besides holding services at the camps and in the various villages where the Marines are billeted, and acting in a general way as the big brothers of the men, they have to censor all mail and serve as the statistical officers of the regiment. At the front they have charge of all burials, collect the bodies, and attend to the matters of record and identification. And more often than not they volunteer to assist the surgeons.

In each of our two regiments there were two chaplains, a Protestant and a Catholic. After the battle was over, all four of them were cited and decorated for heroic action in collecting and burying the dead and assisting the surgeons under fire.

Gradually terror and the realization of defeat began to creep into the hearts of the Boches. Wrote one of the boys:

"Not once in the days of fighting that followed did a German stand up when the Americans got close to him. We've got their number and they know it. I wish I could get over and tell you all about it. I'm so full of stuff I simply can't write the things in a straight-out way.

"You know how I did worry about a pistol and field glasses. Well, it wasn't necessary. I now have the best Zeiss glasses the Imperial German Government could purchase for me, and the splendid new Lauger pistol that I swing at my belt is certainly the finest the Hohenzollerns could provide for an American Army officer.

"In many places they left so fast that clothing, boots, rifles, machine guns and all sorts of booty taken from French towns was left. Every soldier had at least two Boche overcoats for a mattress.

"In one officer's overcoat Lieutenant Blaisdell found a cat-o'-nine-tails, ample evidence of the statement of many prisoners that they were driven time and again to fight."

There were evidences everywhere, during this fighting, of German treachery. Those Prussians were nasty fighters. The following is quoted from the letter of a Quartermaster's Sergeant who talked with a number of our wounded in the hospital:

"If evidence were lacking of ingrained German untrust-worthiness and treachery, the following from the lips of three men, one an officer, would be ample. During the progress of a hot engagement a number of Germans, hands aloft and crying 'Kamerad!' approached a platoon of Marines who, justifiedly assuming it meant surrender, waited for the Germans to come into their lines as pris-oners. When about three hundred yards distant, the first line of Germans suddenly fell flat upon their faces, disclosing that they had been dragging machine guns by means of ropes attached to their belts.

"With these guns the rear lines immediately opened fire and nearly thirty Marines went down before, with a yell of rage, their comrades swept forward, bent upon re-venge. I am happy to state that not a German survived, for those who would have really surrendered when their dastardly ruse failed were bayoneted without mercy.

"As stated, I talked separately with three different Marines at different times, and have no doubt of the truth of the story. When it spreads through the Corps, it will be safe to predict that the Marines will never take a prisoner.

"Can they be blamed? As one man remarked,' A good German is a dead German.' Another said, 'They are like wolves and can only hunt in packs. Get one alone, and he is easy meat.'

"Little of this sounds uplifting, and smacks of cal-loused sensibilities. But the business that brought these men to France is not a refined one. It is kill or be killed, perhaps both, and the duty of each man in the American army is to kill as many of the enemy as may be, before he, in turn, is killed. Likewise it is his duty to study and understand the psychology of the German, and he does it in his crude way, although he might not understand such mental processes by the term psychology.

"An occupation lacking refinement creates unrefined descriptive terms, and the man whose temporary trade is war chooses his own phrases and originates new definitions.

"I will not deny that my nerves are tense with horror at what I have seen, and with pride at what our boys have done, even while my soul is sickened with this closer view of the red monster, War. In the spirit of the men seen to-day, I am moved to greater admiration for their qualities and an abiding faith in our ability to finish as we have begun. Youth of the American army, flower of our young manhood, my hat is off to you! May victory perch upon your banners, and God give you the reward you deserve here and hereafter."

And here is further evidence of German gentleness from the pen of Private James Donohue, a Buffalo boy, who was captured by the enemy and was, I am told, the first American prisoner to escape and make his way back to our lines.

"I attacked with our boys," wrote Donohue, "and ran into a lot of Fritzies. One of them hit me on the head with the butt of his rifle, and when I woke up, I was inside the German lines being dragged before an officer at German headquarters. Every one I passed along the road kicked, jeered, and spit at me.

"When I landed in headquarters, a pompous German officer asked me how many divisions we had in France. I said 'thirty,' but he didn't believe me. A guard was then placed over me, who watched me all night. Just as day was breaking, I was roughly awakened and given an axe and without breakfast I had to cut a lot of brush that was to serve as camouflage for machine guns.

"I was working close to the front lines and American machine gun bullets whistled past me for fair. I had to work all that night. When I tried to snatch even a few minutes of sleep, a husky guard would give me an awful kick with a big hob-nailed boot and I would grab the axe and go to chopping again. I saw three Germans disguised in American uniforms. I was getting so weak from hunger and loss of sleep that I thought I would go under any minute. Finally the guard gave me some black bread and thin, watery soup. I could not get any coffee.

"Afterward they put me to digging trenches to bury dead Germans in. Along with other prisoners we dug long rows, two and three deep, into which it seemed as if they buried the whole German army.

"Finally one night, I found my guard asleep. I walloped him over the head with my pickaxe. He never moved. I ran away through the woods in front and there chanced across some German Red Cross dogs. I found some canteens of water and hunks of bread tied on their backs, which I took.

"All of a sudden I got where shells were bursting everywhere. I had run into a barrage and thought it was all up with me. But I ducked along and suddenly a sentry challenged me. I recognized him as an American and shouted at the top of my voice, 'I am an American. Don't shoot.'

"So he passed me through the lines and that night I slept in the wood inside the lines and reported the next morning."

And so the battle continued, with our boys edging their way slowly ahead in the forest, the ghastly dead lying all about them. Companies that had entered the battle 250 strong dwindled to fifty or sixty with a Sergeant or only a Corporal in command; but with burning eyeballs and drawn faces they fought doggedly on. The Germans brought up reserves and stiffened their resistance. A tremendous and continuous artillery fire was concentrated on the wood, Bouresches, and all the approaches. Gas was poured in, the deadly, insidious yperite, that saturates the clothing and burns the skin and hangs for days in thickets and low places. The strain was beginning to tell.

Gallant as had been the fighting of the Marines in Belleau Wood, it was finally decided that their first operations were not sufficiently decisive. Their progress was too slow and too costly. The Germans were concentrating their forces in the northern half of the woods and it seemed impossible to drive them out and complete the occupation without more thorough artillery support.

On June 9th, accordingly, Sibley received orders to withdraw to give the artillery a chance. Back to the edge of the woods he came, with the ragged remnant of his brave battalion, fighting a rear guard action. Many of them were wounded; some of them had worn their gas masks for eighteen hours at a stretch; they had lived on scanty rations and had enjoyed but little sleep or rest; they were weary, spent, sated with killing; but every man was mad clean through because he could not go on and settle the rest of the German army then and there.

Fifty American and French batteries—some 200 guns in all—then let loose an infernal fire on the woods. The infantry action had given the artillery a chance to get thoroughly ready for this storm of fire. And they battered the last spark of fighting spirit out of the Huns.

On the 10th, after hours of bombardment, Major Hughes went in with part of his battalion and reported that the woods had been reduced. He and Wise worked steadily up from Sibley's former position and extended the line in the wood farther to the north. Hughes himself was later gassed and had to come out.

The Germans had tried attack after attack to drive the Marines out but without success. Now they were up against a more serious situation. The combined artillery and infantry attack was too much for them. It must not be supposed, however, that there was any lack of resistance. The enemy still operated numerous machine gun nests in well selected positions, many of them cleverly camouflaged, which our shells had missed. And so the hand-to-hand fighting was resumed, though against less frightful odds.

Early on the morning of the 10th the Marines started in again, with the artillery fire sweeping the woods ahead of them, and began to clean out the rest of those machine guns with rifle, hand grenade, and bayonet. They partially surrounded the woods and subjected the flanks of the German defenders to a taste of their own medicine. The Boches began to flee, and some of them ran into their own machine gun fire. They were cut up and slaughtered. They began surrendering in groups.

On that day our line was advanced two-thirds of a mile on a 600-yard front, and all but the upper portion of the wood was cleared of Germans. And behind our men came the Engineers, constructing a strong position.

Our casualties on that day were heavy, but if it was bad for us it was inferno for the Boche. Hundreds of Germans were slain, and those that were captured were heartily glad it was over. The wood which they had chosen as an impregnable fastness had proved to be a death trap. We took 300 prisoners that day, and found that many of them belonged to the Fifth German Guard Division, including the crack Queen Elizabeth Regiment.

On the same day—the 10th—the Germans launched an attack in force to regain Bouresches. It was well planned and was executed by fresh troops. A dark, cloudy night had aided their preparations, but they were expected. The Americans had the northern side of the town lined with machine guns and heavier guns were trained on the railroad embankment over which the Germans must come.

Following the usual artillery preparation they advanced in close formation. At the edge of the town they were met by the sting of the machine gun fire and were checked with heavy losses. Then our artillery laid down a thick barrage behind their advanced line, preventing the bringing up of reinforcements. They could neither advance nor retreat; they were caught between two destructive fires. Gradually the barrage was lowered upon their advance line and their position became a slaughter pen. Those who got into town never got out again and the rest were driven back to their lines. The well organized attack was simply crumpled up and wiped out. We had very few casualties and took fifty men captive and one officer.

In Belleau Wood the advance after the 10th was slow but continuous behind an effective barrage. Almost imperceptibly our line was pushed forward among the trees, like water eating its way into a snow bank. As fast as they advanced the Marines dug in and stuck, though constantly shelled and gassed. There was less hand-to-hand fighting now, but casualties on both sides were numerous and the Marines continued to capture prisoners and machine guns.

Between June 6th and 15th six main attacks were made against the woods and nine counter-attacks were repulsed. The Germans tried to filter in from the left but were beaten off. Bouresches was subjected to an aerial bombardment, but the Marines stuck there, too. What they have they hold.

Private F. E. Steck of Camden, N. J., remembers this period rather vividly, for it was then he was wounded. Steck's company did not take part in the attack on Belleau Wood until June 11th, but they were not all idle while in reserve. He and two sergeants succeeded in sneaking out at night and bringing back wounded Marines they found in that area. Private Steck doesn't know whether his officers learned of these nightly "desertions." The trio succeeded, however, in rescuing many companions in this manner.

"We came across a German officer seated comfortably with his knees crossed," Steck relates. "Before him was spread a little field table on which was cake, jam, cookies, and a fine array of food. A knife and fork was in either hand.

"Beside the officer was seated a large, bulky Sergeant who had been knitting socks. The darning needles were still between his fingers. Both their heads had been blown off by a large shell.

"We went into hot fighting on June 11th at 2 A. M. A few hours before I had been on a detail that was bringing up hot coffee from the rear.

"Hand grenades were distributed and then Captain L. W. Williams lined us up in combat formation. Soon we were going single file through the woods and charging across the open area to where the Germans were secluded in their holes.

"My duties were to load a Chauchat or French automatic rifle. You could run about nine steps and then another clip would have to be inserted. Bullets slit my canteen, hit my scabbard, and two or three went through my trousers without touching me. We had advanced in triangle formation about half a mile. I was in the front end of the 'V' when three machine bullets got me. One went into the neck, another in my left shoulder, and the third in my arm.

"I tried to keep on in assisting the operation of the automatic but the blood came up in my throat. I forced my way back and hid in a shell hole in the woods until a little Marine found me. This fellow dragged me five hundred yards on his shoulder to a first-aid dugout. There a shelter-half was used as a stretcher and I was taken back to a larger dressing station."

Private John C. Geiger's company was also one of those that were held in reserve during the first few days of the fighting, but when they got their chance they went to it as though afraid that their comrades had left them no Germans to kill. It was the attack of June 10th which they took a leading part in, and at last they found themselves entering the blood-soaked wood. They surged forward in a two-wave formation at five-pace intervals, but they were an impatient bunch and the waves did not last long in the wood. It was impossible to hold the second wave back and the attacking force soon became one line of fierce fighting men, shooting, bayoneting, and hurling grenades wherever the Boches dared show themselves.

"Our men were yelling as if they were in a football game. You heard just one cry from the Germans—that was 'Kamerad,'" Geiger declared. "We crossed an open space of nearly a mile when we discovered that we had hit the Germans' second line trench.

"Still we kept going. Of the twenty-five who were with me, only four remained.

"Suddenly we spotted a machine gun. Without a thought the four of us started to charge it. Two of the men were killed immediately. I was shot in the right leg. The last man escaped. He told other Marines of the machine gun and in a few minutes a second and bigger advance was made. They surrounded the gun and the crew wanted to surrender. But there's not much use taking as prisoners men who fire at you until they see they are overpowered. I don't remember any prisoners walking back from that crowd.

"I lay wounded for nearly an hour. For a while I hardly dared to breathe. I was right in line with the machine gun's fire.

"The bullets sped past my ears so closely that I couldn't hear them whizz or buzz. There was nothing but a loud 'Crackety-crack-crack' as they went by. It was just like having your head near the muzzle of the gun.

"Soon the camouflage, consisting of high weeds around me, was shot away. Fortunately the machine gun tried for another target about that time and ceased firing in my direction. I tried to crawl off but couldn't make it very far.

"I heard a German crying piteously 'Wasser, wasser.' It was a fellow I had seen shooting at the Marines a few minutes before.

"I tried to get near him but couldn't make it. I had no water but did have about eight inches of blade that I wanted to present to him.

"Then came a scene I shall never forget. This spot was pretty well abandoned now. The heavy action had moved forward and the Germans were still being pursued.

"I heard occasional revolver shots and through the weeds saw a Hun running about the field shooting wounded Marines. Never before did a man look so like a devil to me and I shall never forget the fiendish glare with which he went about his mission.

"It was not long before five Marines came up. They wanted to carry me off but I told them of the fellow who had been shooting our wounded. Later they returned with that devil's automatic."

Geiger was carried back until hospital men with stretchers appeared. His wound cost him his right foot.

"Shooting Germans is heap more fun than shooting rabbits," says Geiger. "You never could tell what was going to happen. We captured one machine gun and turned it on the Germans until the ammunition was exhausted.

"But I want to give credit to those hospital corps men of the Navy, who worked with the Marines. Those fellows deserve a gold medal or the highest award they can receive. Why, before we could reach our objectives they were right out on the field picking up and tagging the wounded. They didn't mind the danger and did their duty without protection of any kind. They were unarmed and could not shoot a German if they did run across one.

"There was one fellow we knew as 'Little Ol' Pewee' Jones. On June 8, 'Pewee' had his clothes almost shot off but he escaped without serious injury. After a few hours he did get hit badly in the arm but he refused aid and went back to the dressing station alone laughing and cussing the Germans in the same breath.

"It was 'Pewee's' everlasting good spirits and bandying that kept his co-workers and every one he came in contact with in the best of humour.

"Others who deserve worthy mention, too, are men known to me only as First-Class Pharmacist's Mate Tibbets, Second-Class Pharmacist's Mate Israel, and two of their assistants, Russell and Turner."

Private Fank Damron, who was also wounded about this time, gives another glimpse of the fighting in a letter home.

"On the morning of the 13th we saw a German lying ahead of us a few yards. We brought him in. He must have had twenty-five wounds in his arms and legs without being hit in a vital spot.

"This fellow told us that the Prussian Guards were coming and it was but a short time before the information had been relayed back and had reached our leaders.

"And that night they attacked. Let me say right at the start they didn't budge us back an inch. The reception they were given made what few were left forsake all desire for further attacks.

"But those Heinies gave us everything they had by way of artillery fire. And they are good at it, too. Those fellows can place a shell in your hat five miles away.

"That action certainly was hell. We counter-attacked right at the start. It wasn't but a short time when shrapnel got me in the left foot and put me out of action.

"Fellows near by bound up my leg with a belt and made a litter out of a blanket and tree branches. But that broke. I was hours and hours getting back to the dressing station. But two days later the amputation had been made and I was on the road to recovery."

On June 11th the report came in that the enemy's machine gun fire had been practically silenced and he was making a last stand at the northern end of the wood. So far, so good, but our progress was now a mere crawl against concentrated resistance and the fight was not over by any means. The enemy was still supported by the guns at Torcy and our men were under constant fire.

Then the Germans, realizing the seriousness of the situation, resolved to make one last desperate effort to regain what they had lost. Reserves were brought up, including an entirely fresh division, and their forces were strongly concentrated along the whole Belleau Wood front. On June 13th they attacked with stubborn fury. Their orders were to retake Belleau Wood and Bouresches at all costs, and God knows they tried. But that depleted line of Marines, backed now by artillery, still held fast. Held? Nay, worn down and decimated as they were by nearly two weeks of bitter fighting, they counter-attacked, and foot by foot, day by day, they pressed the Prussians back.

For days the Marines kept up that steady, unremitting grind, that constant battering at the German gates. They seemed not to know when they were overwhelmed and beaten. Then, on June 18th, their fury flamed out again. There was a scalding artillery shower from the American guns by way of preface, a quick drive across the open behind a barrage, and then the Marines fell tooth and nail upon the town of Torcy. It was a short and merry battle. The crossroads below Torcy were taken at a rush and the troublesome German batteries behind the town were silenced.

On the 19th a heavy barrage tore up the woods and Marine rifles and bayonets proceeded to complete the job. By the 24th the last German was

cleared out of the main part of Belleau Wood—or
was killed—but it was not until the 26th that the
battle was over.   On that day Major Shearer of the
Sixth was transferred to the command of a battalion
of the Fifth and attacked the last bit of woods held
by the enemy, which lay like a small green island
to the north of Belleau Wood proper.   He took 500
prisoners there, besides machine guns and other
booty, and the last of that formerly victorious German army, smitten hip and thigh, was driven from
cover and forced to fall back to a new line.

Before leaving the dismal waste that was once
Belleau Wood, now haunted by the memories of
brave and fallen comrades, I have one more story
to retell.   It is another dog story, and it was told
by one of those cheerful ruffians who have been
getting their broken bodies mended at the Brooklyn Naval Hospital.   This fellow has had a close
shave, but American surgical skill has pulled him
through.

He took part in some of the hottest fighting in
Belleau Wood and it took more than one piece of
German metal to make him quit.   The first wound
didn't bother him much—"just a scratch in the leg,
and besides we needed every man and in the excitement I didn't care."   So he kept on going until a
piece of shell shattered the bone in his right leg below
the knee.   That stopped him.   He did try to crawl,
but weak from loss of blood and pain he finally gave
it up, waiting for some one to find him and carry him
in.   The "scratch" had been a shell wound where a

big chunk of flesh had been torn from the muscular tissue of his left leg, but in the excitement he hadn't known.

He lay for many hours—a whole day and night they told him later at the hospital—when he felt something pushing against his shoulder. He shut his eyes tight because he thought it might be a Heinie. Then something warm and moist licked his cheek and travelled down toward his lacerated leg, and he looked. His own particular buddie wouldn't have been a more welcome sight than that Red Cross dog.

The dog was a big one and a mongrel. "They don't use any particular breed so far as I could notice," explained the Marine. "He was just a dog, but he sure had learned his work."

He came up to the Marine now, placing himself in such position that the wounded man could see the canteen on his back. The Marine, parched and burning, needed no second invitation but detached the canteen and took a long drink, and then replaced it. He had been without water so long and he was afire with fever and the water was wonderful, so wonderful that he just dropped back satisfied; but the Red Cross dog wasn't satisfied. He had come to do a certain thing and he knew his duty as well as any soldier in the line. He kept pushing against the wounded man's shoulder until he just had to listen. The Marine said "listen" because it seemed almost as if the dog talked to him and said "Come on, buck up, you've got to get out of this."

And the Marine did buck up. He grabbed the dog's tail with one hand and with the other and his useful knee he crawled forward at the dog's leading. But it was slow going and finally he had to give up in despair. The pain was too much, and he had to quit. But the dog didn't quit. He went off at a trot and after a time returned with two Red Cross stretcher men, who carried the Marine to the dressing station.

When the Marine was made comfortable his first thought was very naturally of his rescuer. His surprise was very great when he found that the dog would pay no attention to him.

"That's the way they're trained," it was explained to him. "They pay no attention to any man unless he is wounded and then only to bring him into safety. They go out time after time under shell fire bringing in the wounded, or leading the stretcher men to them, but when they have done that they aren't interested in the wounded any more.

"Another thing they have learned is never to eat anything except food that is given to them by their masters in the dressing station. They are taught to be suspicious of food, for earlier in the war some Red Cross dogs were poisoned."

"They sure are wonderful," the Marine says. "I wish I could have brought that dog home with me, but of course he's enlisted for the term of the war, and had to stay in France."

The action which centred about Belleau Wood and Bouresches, and which had for its object the

relieving of the menacing German pressure northwest of Château-Thierry, may be said to have
been brought to a close on July 1st, when men of
the Ninth and 23rd Infantry of our Division took
the town of Vaux behind a barrage of American
artillery fire.

Vaux lies on the Metz-to-Paris Road about two
miles east of Triangle farm and half way to Château-
Thierry. (See Diagram 2.) Its capture and that
of the Bois de la Marette were necessary to straighten
the line and to free the Metz-to-Paris Road of the
danger of a German attack. The American lines
were rather too far advanced on the left to make the
position secure, and what amounted to a small salient
had to be wiped out. With this removed, Château-
Thierry, the Bois de Belleau, and the road to Paris
were relatively safe.

The task was given to the two regiments of Infantry, which had hitherto seen but little action. They
had been merely holding their section of the line and
serving as a barrier across the threatened road. The
capture of Vaux was not spectacular, but was a
cleanly done job from a military point of view. Our
guns were now in position in force, and there was
perfect artillery preparation, such as had not been
possible in the earlier fighting. Following a thoroughly effective barrage, the Infantry took their
objectives almost without loss, and the work for
which our division had been thrown in was completed.

The Marine Brigade was soon withdrawn to a

quiet place for a period of hard-earned rest, to mend battered heads and limbs, to fill the gaps in the ranks with replacements, and to prepare for the next job. In about two weeks it was "Marines to the front!" again.

CHAPTER XI

"They Fought Like Fiends"

ONE prisoner that we took at Belleau Wood stated that the impression had been created among his comrades that all the Americans had become drunk before going into battle, for no men in their sober senses could have fought so like fiends. Well, they weren't drunk, but they did fight like fiends, and so many of them performed prodigious deeds of personal valour that the story of them is bewildering. I want to tell some of these individual stories, for they are thrilling in themselves and they give a sort of mosaic picture of the battle in the woods. But when I glance over the list of the citations which our Marines received I find it difficult to make a selection. There are so many of them, of almost equal importance, and I dislike to mention one brave man and not another. The best I can do is to recount a few of these true tales that particularly gripped me by reason of their dramatic quality, hoping that it will be understood that there are dozens of others of which these are merely a sample.

First let me tell something about one of our old-timers, one of the most noteworthy characters of our Corps—Sergeant Major John Quick. He is a Marine of some thirty years' standing, and what he doesn't know about the service must be a matter of small importance.   In 1898 he signalled to the fleet from an exposed hilltop in Cuba with hundreds of Spanish rifles firing at him, and for that act he received a Medal of Honour.   In 1914 it was Quick who hoisted the Stars and Stripes above the Hotel Terminal in Vera Cruz when every window sill and roof parapet was the gun rest of a Mexican sniper.   He helped to whip our new Marines into shape at Quantico and to keep the wheels oiled at Château-Thierry.   Then, when there was need for heroism of a rare kind combined with a quick brain and steady nerves, it was Quick who, though supposed to be at regimental headquarters with Evans, doing clerical and executive work behind the lines, rose up from the earth and took into Bouresches that truck-load of ammunition along a road swept by artillery and machine gun fire.   He thereby "relieved a critical situation," in the words of the order citing him for bravery, and he received the Distinguished Service Cross.

I don't know what to think of John Quick.   I think he must carry a rabbit's foot or some other amulet about with him, for he has repeatedly risked his life in the most hazardous undertakings and he has usually come through without a scratch.   In fact, I believe he has never been seriously wounded. They say the only time he ever got hurt was at the end of a long march in the Philippines to rescue a detachment of Americans who had been cut off. Nearly dead with exhaustion and hunger, he fell over a precipice into a river. A native pulled him out and he spent the next two months in the hospital.

Quick is the sort of man we like to put in with the young recruits, for he is a living example of what a Marine ought to be. He is the Mulvaney of our Corps. Now he has returned to America to resign. We in the Corps are mournful, but Quick has finished his job, he deserves his rest.

Then there is another picturesque old-timer that I must tell about—First Sergeant Dan Daly of the machine gun company of the Sixth. He enlisted in January, 1899. He first distinguished himself during the Boxer Rebellion in China when, on the night of July 15, 1900, he volunteered to remain alone under fire in a bastion in Peking, which he held until aid came. For this act and for his conduct during the siege of Peking and the battle of August 14th, he was awarded the Congressional Medal of Honour. During the outbreak in Haiti, under odds of ten to one, he led a squad of Marines against Fort Dipitie on October 24, 1915. The men were in pitch darkness and were obliged to wait until daybreak, when they advanced under heavy fire. Their steady shooting and cool discipline alarmed and disorganized the Cacos. In a short time they had captured the fort and set it on fire. For this Daly was awarded his second medal. When the Marines landed at Vera Cruz Sergeant Daly inspired his men to limitless daring, and for his he was recommended for a third medal.

Daly went to France with us and he fought there with all his old-time fire. Boches meant no more

to him than Mexicans.   In Belleau Wood he located
a machine gun and took it single-handed, charging
its crew with a yell and killing most of them before
they could put up a fight.   For that and for some
other little matters General Pershing sent him a
Distinguished Service Cross, the citation reading as
follows:

"Sergeant Daly repeatedly performed deeds of heroism
and great service on June 5, 1918.   At the risk of his life
he extinguished a fire in an ammunition dump at Lucy-
le-Bocage.   On June 7, 1918, while his position was under
violent bombardment, he visited all the gun crews of his
company, then posted over a wide portion of the front,
to cheer his men.   On June 10, 1918, he attempted an
enemy machine gun emplacement unassisted and captured
it by use of hand grenades and his automatic pistol.
On the same day, during the German attack on Bouresches,
he brought in wounded under fire."

If you can picture Dan Daly doing these things
there in the smoke and uproar of battle, with his
comrades falling on every hand, you may be able
to get some conception of what the fighting was like,
for there were hundreds of our fellows doing just
that sort of thing.

Captain Burns of the 74th Company offers a good
example of the spirit of the Marines.   He also got
after a machine gun nest and had both legs shot off.
Later I saw him in the hospital.   He was smoking
a cigarette, and he blithely remarked, "No more toe
dancing for me, I guess."   I regret to say that he did
not recover.

I have already mentioned Captain Duncan of the 96th Company, who was ever a source of inspiration to his men and who led the advance against Bouresches with his pipe in his mouth. He died with his face to the enemy, and if you never saw anything but the laconic citation which recounted his act, you would never know what a splendid type of American hero he was. "Captain Donald Duncan of St. Joseph, Mo., on the night of June 6th, courageously led his men through the machine gun fire in the street fighting which resulted in the capture of the village of Bouresches. He was killed while the town was taken."

Major Berry of the Fifth was awarded the Distinguished Service Cross by General Pershing, and his citation is almost as brief and unemotional as that of Duncan. "Major Benjamin S. Berry led his men in a gallant attack across open ground and into the Bois de Belleau, northeast of Château-Thierry, on the afternoon of June 6th, inspiring them to deeds of valour by his example. When he reached the edge of the woods, he fell, severely wounded. Nevertheless, he arose and made a final dash of thirty yards through a storm of bullets and reached again the first wave of his command before yielding to exhaustion from his injury."

I briefly mention these few instances at the outset to give an idea of the sort of things the officers did. Some of the most picturesque exploits, however, were accomplished by privates. The story of Private Henry Lennert is one of the best. Lennert was captured by the Germans and was held in an officers' dugout for three days. He wondered why he was not sent to the rear or set to work like most of the prisoners. The captain of the company into whose clutches he had fallen spoke English, and occasionally dropped in to chat with Lennert. He asked repeatedly what sort of treatment was accorded to German prisoners, whether they were summarily shot as had been reported.

"Shot?" responded Lennert. "Why, no; they are given a good feed and sent to a quiet place."

On the third night, after a good deal of this sort of questioning, the Captain asked, "Could you get us safe into the American lines if we were to surrender?"

"Sure," replied Lennert. "Easy."

"Then come with me," said the Captain.

The Marine was led out of his dugout, and there in the darkness he beheld what appeared to be the entire company lined up. He wondered whether it could be a firing squad, or whether some new form of German trickery had been invented, but the Captain showed him that their arms had been thrown down and bade him lead the way. Lennert picked up a few souvenirs and set forth toward the American lines.

At length he was challenged by an outpost.

"Who goes there?"

"A Marine," replied Lennert, "with a bunch of recruits that want to sign up."

The American guard advanced and Lennert led

proudly into the lines eighty German prisoners including the Captain and four other officers.

One of our most daring young athletes was Carleton Burr. I wish I could remember all the stories they told of him. He had been in the American Ambulance for about a year, when he came home and got a commission in the Marines. He trained at Quantico and was transferred to the first outfit of the Sixth that went across. Because of his initiative and daring he was made intelligence officer of the First Battalion and achieved some remarkable successes at patrol work while we were in the trenches. But hard luck came to him when we went in at Château-Thierry. He was gassed at Belleau Wood about June 5th and was evacuated to the rear. He knew we were fighting and was crazy to get into it. About July 21st he managed to get out of the hospital and rejoined his regiment at Soissons. Forty-five minutes after he went in he was killed by a shell. Not all our dare-devils bear charmed lives.

From various brief reports of individual valour that have come back to us I have culled a few that give an idea of the fighting in the wood. Corporal Christie Collopy of Spring City, Pa., kept his group under cover and then went out alone with hand grenades and routed an enemy machine gun crew. Gunnery Sergeant Grover C. Conrad of Lexington, N. C., when his commander was wounded and the strength of his platoon was reduced to himself and five men, took charge, advanced, and silenced an enemy machine gun. Private Clarence W. Kelly of

Oil City, Pa., led a rush into a German machine gun position, himself accounting for six of the enemy. Corporal Earl F. Miller of Chattanooga, Tenn., went out alone after a German sniper in a tree whom he killed with a well thrown hand grenade. Private Charles McGarland, a baseball player, by himself hand-grenaded the enemy out of two machine gun positions. Private Walter J. Ball of Roxbury, Mass., crept to within twenty yards of a German sniper and got him with an automatic rifle. And such instances could be multiplied by the score.

On June 9th the French, who were holding a small wood on our left, called for aid, as the Lieutenant in command had only twenty men left and the Germans were advancing to attack. Lieutenant Robert Blake of Berkeley, Cal., responded promptly with twelve men from the American front line. When they arrived at the French position the Germans were but 200 yards away, coming in three waves, supported by machine guns. A wheat field was immediately in front and screened the Germans, so that the handful of Marines had to stand on their feet in a withering fire, blazing away with their rifles. By reason of their cool and accurate fire they soon had the Germans running back. Many of the party were wounded and all have received the Croix de Guerre.

An amusing story is told of Captain Alphonse De Carre of Washington, who went forward with his company to the support of his Lieutenant Colonel. On the way he kept bumping into groups of Germans, utterly terrified, who had been passed in the advance. Had they been properly officered, these Germans might have attacked the advanced American troops from the rear and partially surrounded them, but De Carre supposed they were prisoners who had been left behind by his commander, and he coolly gathered in 164 of them and sent them to the rear before he learned the truth about them.

Private Frank Cronewett of Monrovia, Cal., was an ambulance driver loaned to the American troops by the French army. He ran his ambulance along a road full of shell holes between Bouresches and Coupru when it was being gassed. He took off his mask to see the way better and was burned about the eyes and face, but kept to his work of transporting the wounded. On his way back with an empty ambulance on one trip he had a French soldier on the front seat with him. A shell exploded in the road, wounding his companion. He stopped the ambulance, put the wounded soldier inside, took him to the hospital, where he had a cut in his own head dressed, and then reported for duty and continued in service.

There are, altogether, several hundred citations on file—that is, recommendations for bravery on the battlefield. Over 500 of these give the names of individual heros of the Battle of Belleau Wood. One group is printed at the end of this volume. Many of these men won decorations, and a mere list of them would be too long to include here. They tell of officers who led desperate attacks against odds; of wounded officers who refused to leave their commands and go to the rear; of non-coms. who took charge of platoons and led them on in the wood after all the officers had been killed or wounded; of men who brought out wounded officers and comrades under fire; of runners, sometimes wounded, who braved death a hundred times a day carrying messages under fire; of drivers who brought up ammunition and supplies through a storm of shells and machine gun bullets; of non-coms., privates, and members of the Medical Corps who dressed the wounds of the fallen under fire; of men who continued operating machine guns single handed after all their comrades had fallen; of severely wounded men who walked to the rear to spare the services of the stretcher bearers; of men who displayed exceptional courage and dash in charging machine gun nests. It sometimes seems as though the entire brigade must have been individually cited; indeed, the Marine who did not exhibit personal heroism of a high order in those days was the exception. And there was Private Morris Fleitz who drove battered Elizabeth Ford all over the place, through a spray of shrapnel and bullets, carrying ammunition and rations to exposed points.

CHAPTER XII

"Le Bois de la Brigade de Marine"

A REGIMENTAL or brigade officer has the advantage of being able to view an engagement in its entirety, while the men in the thick of the fighting know only what is going on in their immediate neighbourhood. That is why so many of the letters from the front are fragmentary and give but a sectional view of the great movements of the war. Nevertheless, most of us, because we have personal friends at the front, are vitally interested in knowing something of what the individual soldier accomplishes and suffers, what he is thinking about and how he feels. From the newspapers we learn how the battle goes; it is only from the individual soldier that we can learn how the war appears to the man who is doing the fighting.

For this reason I venture to present one more letter from a Marine in France before proceeding with the rest of my story. It is one of the most interesting letters I have seen and I offer it in full because it tells the whole story of Belleau Wood from the restricted but intense viewpoint of the man behind the bayonet. It was written by Private Hiram B. Pottinger of the 76th Company, Sixth Regiment, to his mother in St. Louis.

171

"I wrote you a card yesterday telling you we had gone over the top. Well, we sure went over the top and we had some battle. I will tell you the story as near as I can.

"It happened early in the morning and before daylight we were all lined up behind our lines. In front of us lay a large open field and in front of that a thickly wooded hill. That was where we were going. We all had kind of a funny feeling, but we laid back there smoking and telling jokes while we waited for the order to form. During all that time our artillery was throwing a barrage into the woods ahead of us, and believe me they were sure tearing things up, too.

"Well, at daylight we commenced to form. Our company was in about the fourth or fifth wave and then the advance started. I would give anything for a picture of those 'leathernecks' that morning going across that field, for we were behind and could get a good view of it.

"Across the field we went and up the hill and over, but the Germans never put up much of a fight. I guess the shell fire was too much for them and they retreated. We took positions at the edge of the woods and stayed there all day. The next day was the day of the fighting in which our company took a big part—we took a wood which had formerly been known as the 'Machine Gun Nest,' 'Death Valley' and all such names as that, and none of the names were too good for it.

"The first sight that struck my eyes when our little platoon started through the woods was a place where the Germans had shot liquid fire and the ground and woods all around were scorched black. In the middle of this were men's bodies all charred and some of their faces almost burned off. A little farther on I stumbled over the body of a man who must have been killed a month before. I tell you such sights as that gives you a sick feeling if you have seen nothing like it before, but I soon forgot them, for it was then we spied the Boches.

"They were placing a machine gun to turn it on us, but they never did get it placed, for we let out a yell and fired into them, wiping all of them from the gun, and in a second we had the gun in our hands.

"They must have thought from the way we were shooting and yelling that the whole American army was coming through the woods, for they blew a call to either retreat or surrender and they came running out of the woods with their hands up, yelling, 'Kamerad, Kamerad,' and we took an awful mob of prisoners right there.

"One of our men could speak German and he got the lay of everything from a prisoner who was scared to death. We then advanced on their flank so as to come up behind them, and that we did. We caught four or five bunches of them in the act of swinging their machine guns on us, but our eyes and rifles were too quick for them and we wiped more than one crew away from their guns. That was our main watch-out, machine guns. We got about half way through the woods and started raising hell in general; we killed Boches like rabbits; they would not fight us hand to hand. Seeing their machine gun was lost, they threw up their hands and yelled 'Kamerad—mercy.' One guy threw a whole bundle of hand grenades at us and then yelled 'mercy.' He is still laying up there, I guess.

"We took their machine guns and turned them on the Boches as we advanced through the woods, also their grenades and pistols. We had nothing of our own except our rifles and bayonets, but that was enough for them, for the sight of our bayonets made them shout 'Kamerad.' It was then that the old saying about your rifle being your best friend came true, for they were sure our best friends that day.

"At last we reached our objective. It was a bunch of great big rocks, but we never stopped. We stormed the rocks, but all we found was a lot of dead Huns. If they would have let us go on we would have gone clear to Berlin, but when we reached our objective we had to stop.

"We then started to dig in. We brought up the machine guns we had captured and put them on the line with us; then in a little while our own guns got up on the line and we were pretty well fixed for the counter-attack we expected. But we were not there two hours until they started shelling us and then, after not losing a single man in the attack, one was killed and two wounded, including one Lieutenant, by shell fire. But it only lasted about two hours. Then it quieted down, but we kept on digging and dug down underneath the rock and made regular dugouts for ourselves. Everything went well until the next afternoon and then hell started.

"They gave us a bombardment which lasted about five or six hours, which none of us will ever forget as long as we live. It tore the woods all to thunder, the trees looked as though somebody had cut them down with a scythe. All that afternoon the ground just rocked under shell fire, and the gas was so thick at times you could not see two feet in front of you. By night about half the platoon was killed or wounded, and it did not look as if any of us had a chance to get out alive, but we stayed, and the bombardment kept right on, and about midnight it quieted down a little and over they came with a counter-attack, but as you might know, sleeping was out of the question, and we saw them coming, although it was pitch dark.

"As the Lord would have it, not one of our machine guns had been hit, and when they started over, we crawled up out of our holes and pumped enough iron into them to kill the whole German army. But it only lasted a few minutes, for the Huns threw up a call for a barrage and retreated, and we had to hunt our holes once more, for the shells started dropping by the thousands. The whole end of my rifle was blown off by shrapnel, and my bayonet was shattered into a million pieces. It was pretty tough to lose that rifle, too, after carrying it so far, but I had to hunt another one.

"Until we were relieved the days we spent were days of hell, for the bombardment kept right on, and you were taking your life in your hands when you left your hole. Why, the concussion of the air made by some of those high explosives just knocked the wind out of me, and I was buried beneath the earth three times.

"We never thought much about eating or sleeping, for they tried an attack almost every night. We were gassed so much that we had to wear our masks a good part of the time, but we held our ground and never gave an inch, and drove back every attack they tried to make. I went after rations one night (there were three of us), and coming back through the woods we were caught in a barrage. We threw down our sacks and jumped into a hole, and had hardly done that when a shell hit just a few feet away. A piece of shrapnel about a cubic inch in size went clear through the sack of bread and grazed my hand, knocking a hunk of flesh off, but it never amounted to anything.

"By the time we were relieved our platoon had dwindled down to about twenty-odd men, and we came back leaving our best pals up there. When we came out we brought along the machine guns we had captured, and are sending the finest one to Major General Barnett, commander of the Marine Corps. Our one little platoon captured about (censored) prisoners, and I do not know how many machine guns.

"But we won. We advanced about three miles and held everything we took and found out we were not fighting fighters, but cowards, who have to rely on artillery and machine guns to do their fighting."

Before passing on to the subsequent activities of the Marines in France it may be well to survey the Battle of Belleau Wood in its entirety, that it may appear in its true proportions in relation to the rest of the war in general and the strategy of the Marne salient in particular. Just what did this month of bloody fighting accomplish, with its terrific losses in our ranks? What were its strategic and moral results?

In the first place, the German rush toward Paris was definitely and finally stopped. The day before the Marines went in the Germans had advanced six miles against the weakening resistance of the French. After that they advanced not a step. It is not on my own authority that I make the assertion that the Marines saved Paris. M. Clemenceau said so; the Parisians said so; it was generously admitted by the French commanders. That was the one outstanding result of our effort. The fact received official recognition in various communications and orders, one of the most interesting of which I present herewith:

Translation

With Army Staff.

6930/2   Army H.Q., June 30th, 1918.

ORDER

In view of the brilliant conduct of the 4th Brigade of the 2nd U. S. Division, which in a spirited fight took Bouresches and the important strong point of Belleau Wood, stubbornly defended by a large enemy force, the General commanding the VIth Army orders that henceforth, in all official papers, the Bois de Belleau shall be named "Bois de la Brigade de Marine."

Division General Degoutte,
Commanding VIth Army.

(Signed)   DEGOUTTE.

The strategic situation of the lines at the rounded point of the salient created by the German drive was much improved by the action. In fact, a line was established which had been virtually non-existent. With the French coöperating on the left, the Americans forced the German line back two kilometres on an eight-kilometre front. At the end of the action we held a strong line which included the strategic positions at Bussiares Wood, the crossroads south of Torcy, the whole of the Bois de Belleau, Bouresches, and Vaux, establishing a tenable front from Bussiares to Château-Thierry. (See Diagram 6.)

We took, in that action, some 1,400 prisoners and more than 100 guns, including 77's, machine guns, and small mortars.

We whipped more than four times our weight of Germans, fighting in protected positions and including some of the Kaiser's best. A portion of one American division had two and sometimes three German divisions op-

DIAGRAM 6

The final position of the line after the Battle of Belleau Wood.

posed to it. At first they had in line the Tenth, the 197th, and the 237th, and these were so hard pressed that they had to be reformed after the first few days and the 28th and the crack Fifth Guards Division were thrown in. In other words, the two regiments of Marines used up five divisions of the Germans' finest fighting troops.

All this was officially summed up and recorded for us by General Bundy in one of the many communications which reached us. His order reads as follows:

HEADQUARTERS SECOND DIVISION (Regular),
AMERICAN EXPEDITIONARY FORCES.

France, July 10, 1918.

General Orders No. 41.

After more than a month of continuous fighting, the division has been withdrawn from the first lines. It is with inexpressible pride and satisfaction that your commander recounts your glorious deeds on the field of battle.

In the early days of June, on a front of twenty kilometres, after night marches, and with only the reserve rations which you carried, you stood like a wall around the enemy advance on Paris. For this timely action you have received the thanks of the French people whose homes you saved, and the generous praise of your comrades in arms.

Since the organization of our sector, in the face of strong opposition, you have advanced your lines two kilometres on a front of eight kilometres. You have engaged and defeated with great loss three German divisions, and have occupied the important strong points of the Belleau Woods, Bouresches, and Vaux. You have taken about fourteen hundred prisoners, many machine guns, and much other material. The complete success of the infantry was made possible by the splendid coöperation of the artillery, by the aid and assistance of the engineer and signal troops, by the diligent, watchful care of the medical and supply services, and by the unceasing work of a well-trained staff. All elements of the division have worked together in perfect harmony as a great machine. Amid the dangers and trials of battle, every officer and every man has done well his part. Let the stirring deeds, the hardships, the sacrifices of the past month remain forever a bright spot in our history. Let the sacred memory of our fallen comrades spur us on to renewed efforts to add to the glory of American arms.

(Signed)   OMAR BUNDY,
Major General, N. A.

And finally, the achievement of the United States Marines brought new hope to the people of imperilled France and new confidence to the Allied armies. What they had done was an earnest of what America would continue to do. There in our little section of the far-flung battle line we had given a fair sample of the sort of fighting that might be expected of America at war.

It was like many a football match you have attended, with the game going dead against your side in the second half. The opposing team has recently made a touchdown and the score is in their favour. The ball is in their possession and they are forcing it steadily down the field, five, ten, fifteen yards at a rush. The defence seems to have crumpled. Your team, beaten by superior weight, appears to be all in and there is small hope of regaining the offensive before another score is tallied.

Nearer, nearer to the goal the scrimmage line is pressed. You sit on the bleachers with clenched fists and groan inwardly—perhaps aloud. The game seems lost.

Suddenly from the sidelines, at the command of coach and captain, a substitute back field jumps in to take the places of the worn-out plungers. They are not the veterans of the team, but they are fresh, strong, eager to make good and to save the day.

Again the shock of attack. You watch the line bend, sway, then hold. The new backs plunge into it, fighting like wildcats. Twice more the desperate charge is loosed and twice more the line holds, though perilously near the goal line.

There is a pause; the linesmen do some measuring; the referee raises his hand; the boys at the score board manipulate the letters and figures. A wild cheer goes up from the bleachers. Your side has the ball

again and there is yet hope. The blood races again
through your veins; your benumbed brain is aroused
to new activity. The advance is checked on the
threshold of defeat; the ball is punted out of danger,
and with fresh courage and a new chance your team
begins once more to fight.

That is the way it was there on the Marne in June,
1918. I do not wish to overemphasize the strategic
or tactical importance of the Battle of Belleau Wood,
nor the part the Marines played in the great game of
the war. But unquestionably they did do just what
fresh blood will often do on a football field. They
brought into the conflict new zest, new strength, new
courage. The German advance slowed up and the
whole Allied world took heart. The game had by
no means been won yet, but that heart-breaking rush
down-field was checked by the United States Marines.

They were untried, inexperienced, green in the
grim business of fighting; they were substitutes, if
you will; but when they went in it made all the
difference in the world to the losing side. For it was
then that the French took heart of hope, and with
their new allies at their elbows, they held the baffled
Hun for downs on their five-yard line.

CHAPTER XIII

AT SOISSONS AND AFTER

THE Second Division, to which the Marine Brigade belonged, was now one of the veteran divisions of the American Army in France, and I have seen it stated by correspondents on more than one occasion that, as a fighting unit, it was considered the equal of any division of any army in Europe. For that reason it was not allowed to rest idly on the laurels it had won at Belleau Wood but was repeatedly called upon for hard action up to the very moment of the cessation of hostilities.

In July the Second Division was honoured by Marshal Foch who especially selected it to aid in leading the drive at Villers-Cotterets in the Soissons offensive. Again, in September, Pershing had the Second Division in the van at St. Mihiel. Later, in October, it took part in the attack on BlancMount which relieved the pressure about Rheims. And finally, it participated in the capture of Sedan and the final breaking of the strongest part of the German line.

First, the Franco-American attack on Soissons, an action in which the Marines won no less credit than in the affair at Belleau Wood and which was part of a broader and more important movement.

Undoubtedly the American successes in the Château-Thierry sector encouraged Foch to take the
offensive in July.   Because of the rapidly augmenting
American armies in France he was able to bring up
his splendid French reserves and strike the blow that
placed the German commanders on the defensive and
sounded the death knell to German hopes.   He knew
now that he could count on Americans to fight.   He
used them in that offensive and they did not fail him.

It will be remembered that the drive that menaced
Paris resulted in a deep, U-shaped salient thrust down
from the Chemin-des-Dames to the Marne, its bottom resting on Belleau and Château-Thierry and the
upper ends of the two sides being near Soissons and
Rheims respectively.   Rheims was held strongly
against German attack, but Soissons had been included in the territory won by the drive.   It was at
Soissons, at the upper end of the left-hand side of the
salient (See Diagram I), that Foch decided to launch
the attack which had for its ultimate purpose the
pinching out of the entire salient—a purpose eventually achieved.   Here the French General's superb
strategy completely outwitted the Hun.   He suddenly massed his forces on an apparently inactive
sector of the front and delivered a surprise attack in
great force that drove confusion into the German
armies and started the great withdrawal that proved
so costly to the foe.

The action which began on July 18th had for its
immediate objective the cutting of communications
between Soissons and Château-Thierry, thus leaving

a large part of the German army in a helpless condition. The attack was launched at the Forest of Villers-Cotterets, on the western side of the Marne salient below Soissons. Foch used the French reserves which he had been holding for an offensive, but he also summoned to his aid the available Americans, including the Marines.

The two regiments of Marines, when they were withdrawn from the Château-Thierry sector, were placed under the command of Brigadier General Neville and were taken to La Fère, where they remained for a few days, resting and reorganizing. But they did not enjoy a long period of recuperation. They were summoned by Foch to help in the attack on Soissons and they left La Fère in camions.

In a way Soissons was a bigger affair for the Marines than Belleau Wood, though entirely different in character. They were not required there to stop a German drive single-handed, but they took a not inconspicuous part in the big push that drove the Boche back from the Marne. Both the First and Second American Divisions participated in that attack, with the French Moroccan Division between them—one of the crack divisions of the French Army.

The advance of the Marines to the point of attack was a memorable one. They were en route on motor lorries through the whole of one night, hiked during the greater part of the following day, and then, just as darkness began to fall, set out again. They marched until daylight, rested for only a few minutes, and then went in. The Fifth Regiment arrived at the front on the first day of the attack, July 18th. The Sixth relieved them on the second day.

It was a wonderfully planned surprise attack, and the first day's advance of eight kilometres rendered the German position in the salient untenable and its evacuation inevitable. The part of the Second Division in this offensive was the taking of Beau Repaire Farm and Vierzy in an advance of extraordinary rapidity in the face of a murderous machine gun fire which contested every step of the way. They reached the objective position in front of Tigny at the end of the second day. In this action the First and Second Divisions captured 7,000 prisoners and over 400 pieces of artillery.

I am again indebted to Floyd Gibbons, the correspondent of the *Chicago Tribune*, for a first-hand account of what the Marines did at Villers-Cotterets. Having somewhat recovered from the wounds he received at Belleau Wood, he stuck to the Marines and witnessed their mobilization for the new action. He was, quite unexpectedly, the only American correspondent at that point when Foch launched his big drive.

"The Boche was prepared for an attack to come from that place," said the war correspondent. "He had his Prussian Guards all prepared for it. His planes would come out at night looking for ammunition dumps and men and supplies, but there were none to be found. There was nothing to be seen but a little line of Frenchmen, holding a hastily constructed trench on the edge of the forest.

"The Germans believed the Frenchmen, for sentimental reasons, would strike on July 14th—their national gala day. But they did not. The Germans were puzzled. There was no French movement of ammunition or troops, and they did not appear strong enough to hit.

'So they took the Prussian Guards away and moved them over to the Rheims front on the other side of the salient for the purpose of getting Epernay and Chalons—the second phase of their offensive. They attacked there July 15th.

"When Foch learned the German policy he made the master stroke. From somewhere in the line he took the Second Division, including the Marines, and put them in to fill the gaps here and there. He used them all, too. Besides the division to which the Marines were attached, there was another—the finest in the whole French army. The combination of the two was the greatest compliment that could be given to the Marines by the French people. There were also some Morrocan troops, splendid fighters. These troops, chosen to serve with the Marines, are without a doubt the finest the French have. Altogether some 70,000 men were used.

"The Marines and the French had made some preliminary raids on the German lines and knew the exact strength of the forces that opposed them. I have the order, a slip of paper, that came round on the night of July 17th from the American Commander, saying: 'Men of the First and Second Divisions, this honour comes to you, and see that you respond to it.'

"That night the weather for once played in the Allies' hands. It began to thunder, the lightning came and the skies spit fire. The rain came down like the spray of machine guns.

"While the rain poured down, from every avenue

came two long lines of steel trucks, ammunition wagons, and every sort of conveyance. On either side of the road, marching in single file, were American Marines, infantry, and others. All were moving forward. French cavalry, with the lances, were winding in and out of the trees. Little French tanks, green, yellow, brown, and blue, moved forward like monsters in the dark, guided by fellows walking in the front with Turkish towels wrapped around their shoulders, showing faintly white through the darkness. All moved through the forest of Villers-Cotterets.

"It was 4:35. It would have been hell if the Germans had found out there were 70,000 men in the forest. Poisonous gases would have knocked out thousands of them, the place would have been filled with shrapnel—and that would have been the end of that movement!

"The Marines had plainly the furthest distance to move to get into line, and they had to hurry to get there by the zero hour. Yet—would you believe it—after those poor fellows had been on the march all day long, they moved forward on the double time in order to get there on time.

"Then, preceded by artillery barrages, they swept through village after village, scattering the Boche and cutting his communications by capturing the road between Soissons and Château-Thierry.

"The marching was awful. I talked with one chap who was sitting down to rest. When I asked him what was the matter, he said his feet were all in, and he could not run any further.

" 'I enlisted in the Marines to kill Germans,' he said, 'but I did not think we had to run them to death. I recommend that they give us lassoes.'

"Of course," said Mr. Gibbons, "this is not always the

case. Frequently the Boche will hold his ground fairly well.

"When the attack started, I never saw such spirit in my life. Side by side the infantry fought—one side those little French Moroccans, who are really wonderful fighting men.

"I saw quite a sight when the Boche prisoners came back—a long column of them. We were on the edge of what was once a farm. Eight Boches walked ahead of this column, four abreast in front and four in the rear. They had between them two roughly constructed litters with coverings made of German hairy knapsacks. There was a wounded man on each of these litters. These two fellows, one an American and one a Moroccan, were up there in a half-sitting, half-reclining position, using the hairy knapsacks as pillows. Both appeared to be hit in the arms, and their clothing was covered with blood. Each had a cigarette.

"There was a long line of prisoners following them. It was a curious procession. The American was calling to every one who passed, shouting to this one and that one: 'How do you do, boys?' You see reinforcements were coming forward all the time.

"After a while this procession, led by the litters, moved up to where two American generals were standing. The American, who was smoking his cigarette and shouting greetings, spied the generals and poked his companion in the ribs.

"It was the funniest thing to see those two fellows, up there on the litters, throw their cigarettes away, raise themselves to a sitting position on the litters being carried by the Boches, and bring their good arms to a salute when they arrived in front of the generals—for all the world like stern regimental commanders on parade.

"During this never-to-be-forgotten fight of July 18th, they captured many German 77's and other guns, frequently turning them around and letting them go at the Boches. Marines should never forget July 18th."

It was in this action that Private Elmer Groves of Billings, Mont., emulated the example of some of his comrades at Belleau Wood and brought in a batch of German prisoners single-handed. This is the story as told by George H. Seldes, correspondent of the *Buffalo Express:*

"Groves had lost his company in the confusion of the attack at Villers-Cotterets on July 19th.   He wandered about the battlefield until he heard a gunner firing over a knoll.   Wearily he approached the enemy position, and gaining a point of vantage, plugged his man through the hand.   The German could no longer work the machine gun, so he got his revolver and was about to shoot again when Groves shot him through the head.

"The noise of the duel disturbed other Germans who were weathering the American artillery showers in dugouts.   Groves approached the men and, bombs in hand, called upon the Boches to surrender.   One by one they stumbled up the dugout steps, hands over their heads. Groves asked one of them to bandage his bleeding hand, and then, not knowing where his company was, marched his thirty-five prisoners to regimental headquarters and got a receipt for them.   He was told to go on and have his wound treated."

A letter written by Sergeant K. P. Spencer of Kansas City, Mo., gives an unusually colourful picture of the engagement from the fighter's point of view.   He writes:

"The day the Germans began an offensive on the Château-Thierry-Rheims front we were standing by in a small village in the rear of Château-Thierry.   The offensive began that morning—the next morning we were in trucks riding toward Soissons.   An Allied drive was to begin the following morning, July 18th, and our division was to start the ball rolling.

"After the truck ride came a forced march through one of the largest forests in France—immense trees eighty and ninety feet high on both sides of the road as far as one could see.   It was a narrow road but thousands and thousands of men were going forward over it.   A traffic jam on Grand Avenue couldn't compare with the congested condition of this single road leading through the woods.

"Overhead were dozens of airplanes, all of them Allied (the supremacy of air was necessary to protect and cover the movement of troops).   Filing down the right side of the road were three columns of infantry, down the left two columns; on the right centre a continuous stream of vehicles, machine guns, carts, provision and munition trucks, hundreds of artillery pieces and their caissons; occasionally a general in his auto; large French tanks and British armoured cars, and probably best of all the French cavalry, regiment after regiment, going forward at a trot.   On the left side of the road coming out were trucks, ambulances, wagon trains, and artillery limbers.

"All the allied troops of the world were represented here—the Americans in their khaki; Moroccans and Italians wearing a dirty brown coloured uniform; the

Scots in their kilts; Englishmen and Canadians in their khaki; Irish troops wearing tam-o'-shanters, and the French wearing all the different shades of blue imaginable. Here was a display of colours that outclassed the rainbow.

"About 10 P. M. it began raining and we were soon drenched. After about an hour of sliding and slipping around in the mud we left the main drag and made camp under the trees. It was still raining but we were too tired and sleepy to mind it so were soon asleep. Next morning we were awakened at 4:30 A. M. by the bang, bang of several guns, which was soon followed by thousands of them. I have never heard a barrage that could begin to compare with this one; we were only a couple of hundred yards in front of a six-inch battery and the concussion from these large guns was fearful.

"After two hours of this bombarding, our division, excepting this regiment which was reserve, went over. Little resistance was met. By eleven o'clock the line had been advanced ten kilometres and thousands of German prisoners were being marched back (most of them carrying in our wounded and a few of their own). The third line of Hun artillery was passed that day, hundreds of large guns captured and thousands of machine guns. The attack had been a complete surprise so the Germans had either thrown away everything and started running or had been taken prisoner.

"As reserves we followed the advance. The road was more congested than the night before, if such was possible. Hundreds of tanks, armoured cars, and motorcycle machine guns were going forward. The Germans were on the run—we were to keep them going. Toward night we made camp in the woods and slept. We were to attack the next morning.

"At 4 A. M. the barrage was on and we were soon going forward. The attack was scheduled for 7 A. M. A few minutes before this hour we were formed in two more formations on the top of a small hill about 1,000 yards from the Germans. The Germans were on the reverse side of a hill in front of us. About three kilometres behind them was the edge of a woods, our objective.

"While we were waiting, the Hun artillery and machine gunners got busy and clicked off a few casualties, mostly leg wounds, for they were shooting low. We hadn't waited long until we saw the remainder of the regiment coming up behind us. There must have been six or eight waves of them; perfect lines and at intervals of thirty yards. Behind the second wave was a line of tanks. Oh, what a sight, one that even made you forget the Germans were only a short way off shooting at you.

"This formation soon passed through our own and we followed. The tanks did wonderful work that day clearing out machine gun nests, but they drew much artillery fire which inflicted many casualties on the infantry. The Germans threw up a barrage of high explosives and machine gun bullets but we continued to advance and soon had taken the hill they had occupied. Here we dug in and awaited orders. You should have seen us dig—it was no time at all until every man had a hole of some sort.

"Yes, we dug in and we remained. We gained six kilometres that day and all objectives were taken. That night at 12 o'clock we were relieved and started toward the rear. Since then we have been travelling in a leisurely manner away from the front."

The two letters which follow, dealing with this same adventure, fairly illustrate the cheerful attitude of the average Marine lying wounded in the hospital. Private Kenet Weikal of Middletown, Ohio, writes:

"I have seen and fallen over many dead Germans in the past months. I have also quite a few souvenirs, but have thrown some away. It makes things so heavy to carry around on the different and many hikes, but if ever I return, I'll bring a few back with me. One of the souvenirs I have is a piece of the shrapnel that went into my leg; it's about one inch and one-half long; quite a nice thing. I also have a German belt and several buckles with brass and silver. I had a hard time getting them as the dead German was down in a deep hole and to get to him I had to step all over him. I also have a pocketbook and several marks.

"I was wounded on the 18th, perhaps you know by this time. It was about 9:20 in the morning when our batteries and tanks started and we followed the tanks.

"I was in the fourth wave. The first two waves are much better than the others. After going over for about 600 yards and about 100 yards from a small town which was one of our objectives, I received my wound when two big shrapnel shells exploded beside the squad I was in (the first in the line), receiving it in my leg. The next fellow got his left hand blown off, the next was shell shocked and lost his voice, and so on. I could use all the paper in the 'Y' telling how each of us got wounded or killed. It sure is horrible. It is something that is impossible to express, but there is something humorous. As when we just started over, a high explosive shell lit right behind one fellow on my right, and as you know most of the power of a shell goes before it, so, in this case, it didn't hurt the fellow, but just raised him off the ground about three feet. Then turning around he said: 'That one sure had whiskers!' The same fellow had his bayonet taken away by a big shell. But over here one is taught and drilled to take death with a grin.

"We have captured quite a few of the German machine guns and in every case the men were chained to their guns. Being able to speak a little German myself, I asked a young German wounded who was only eighteen years old, how long he had been in the service. He said his mother had hidden him in the woods for two years and that he had just been at the front two days. There are ever so many cases like this.

"I am still in the hospital at Bordeaux with but few new changes. Yesterday I was given ether, then had my wound sewed up. To-day I am walking around without crutches. They can't keep me down (they can't keep a good man down). Ether is sure awful stuff. When I was coming to I made love to the nurse."

Private Robert U. Neal, 45th Company, Fifth Regiment, wrote as follows to his father, Mr. J. H. Neal of the Committee on Public Information:

"I have reached the base hospital at last in fairly good spirits and am able to hobble around a little, just as a wounded guy should. This is a fine place but just a bit awkward without money—no pay yet, you know.

"Every doggone personal thing that I owned in the way of toilet kit (present from Warren), wallet (present from Uncle Walt), my address book, your pictures, fountain pen, etc., is somewhere out in No Man's Land. You see, Hell was a-poppin' so fast during that attack, that toilet kits and excess baggage just couldn't find a lodgment in my cerebrum a-tall.

"Us Marines and doughboys went over the top O. K.

you know, with the tank fleet leading the procession. We had gone several kilometres when one of the many little machine gun bullets stopped its 'wee-ee' song long enough to rip off my gas mask and tear my shirt open. That little manœuvre swung me around to such an inviting positon that I stopped two more of those sweet singing little hunks of lead with my chest. Luckily they hit my bandoliers and no more than bruised me, although my chest is still pretty sore.

" 'I'll catch up as soon as I can get my breath,' said I to the rear Sergeant at the end of the column. Just then a bold, audacious hunk of an eight-inch heavy skipped through my legs instead of around me as any gentlemanly shell would have done, but who ever heard of a Hun shell acting like a gentleman? So there you have the story of how it happened, dear father.

"Darn! There is a lop-eared son-of-a-gun playing all mother's pieces on the piano. I have counted six so far. This is a punk time for getting homesick.

"We have the use of a good library here, which just about saves my life, the 'Y' to write in, moving pictures, billiard table, shower baths, wash room, regular human chow, and a civilized bunk. All that I really need is a toilet kit and a pay-day. Hope to get both in the near future.

"About half a dozen of my company are down here so I can find some one to chat with. Believe they actually deliver mail here once in a while, so I might get some of your letters. Wonderful thought.

"Hope you and mother are both well and can stand for my living this life of sinful ease for a few weeks."

Of all the literature which this war has produced, I know of nothing more thrilling and vivid, or that more truly expresses the soldier's sensations in battle, than a series of letters written by Sergeant Arthur R. M. Ganoe of the Marines to an old friend, Mr. A. W. Brown of Pittsburgh. They appeared first in the Pittsburgh *Gazette-Times*, and I shall take the liberty of quoting from them at some length. After some preliminary paragraphs on the fighting of the Marines, Sergeant Ganoe continues as follows:

"Then on the evening of July 16th we suddenly pulled stakes and vaulted into camions or French motor trucks. The boys love these vehicles. The springs are so staunch and stiff, the hard seats are so dependable, like boards laid on the round side of overturned beer kegs; and their capacity is so blindly ignored when they are loaded. The comment heaped on the guileless French driver during an all-night ride is so refreshing that you don't get tired in any particular place, just all over. But this time the boys were cheerful during the first stages of agony. Although they had no supper there was quite a bit of singing and 'kidding.' They believed themselves at last on the way to a well-earned and longed-for rest. I had a hunch, but said nothing. If ever men needed a rest and deserved it they did. So it was good to hear these young veterans sing once more! Then, too, their arguments were logical. We had been issued no emergency rations, a prime essential in the movement of troops who leave their field kitchen behind. But such things are accomplished so easily at the last moment.

"All night long as we bumped over the traffic-torn roads off to the right the red reflection of the heavies kept pace with us. And I knew my hunch was right. We were not off to a rest camp. When dawn peeped above the purple horizon we pulled into a little village and crawled out of the camion. We were hungry and thirsty, and oh, so sleepy! And we had a long, long road to foot. It started to rain as we started to hike. The booming of the big guns disillusioned the boys. They were drunk on misery. Yet not one word of protest was uttered.

"A division cannot be moved over one road and expect to arrive on the line in proper formation. All the roads leading to the objective must be utilized. And some parts of the division will be dumped quite a long way from their place in the line. This is to avoid congestion of the main traffic arteries. We were dumped twenty-five kilometres from our destination. So we hiked and hiked, till the road beneath us rose in dusty protest at our ceaseless tramp, tramp, tramp. Toward noon we got some water. Everywhere were American troops. We climbed mountains and descended hills, skirted jungles and ploughed through worse. It stopped raining and the sun came out. Sweat followed suit. Our suits were steaming. Canteens went dry. So did we.

"In the afternoon we struck through a huge wood. Magnificent trees! All the underbrush had been cleared out. It was replaced by shells! Acres on acres were piled high with shells of every calibre!

Most of 'em were made in America. How that sight gladdened our tired minds! And around the edges of this stupendous mountain of death there was the liveliest activity, a subdued excitement that boded ill. American and French ammunition trains came tearing, galloping, whirling in dust-clouds ahead of smoking exhausts, into that trembling woods. With seeming recklessness shells were tossed into the wagons and camions, which departed with fresh haste. A flood of giant trucks steamed into that wood, dumped their loads of ammunition and whirled away for more. We boys tightened our belts and determined to stick around. Something was doing!

"Finally we emerged on the main road. And what a road! It was a nightmare, a thousand bedlams. I've seen the busiest thoroughfares in the world. They were country lanes compared to this road. There was noise, *noise*, and *more noise* worse confounded. It was a Niagara of sound, a mighty diapason that deafened us. The shouting and curses in 'steen different languages, the crunch and grind of wheels, the groan of gears, the crackling of whips, the clang of metal, the pounding of countless horses' hoofs, the chugging of streams of motors and the screams of their many-throated sirens, empty ammunition trains coming and loaded ones going, light artillery and heavy artillery, tanks in platoons, trucks in companies, field kitchens, water wagons, supply trains, ration carts, officers' cars, motorcycles, all fought for space and air in which to make their own peculiar noise vibrate. Every square foot of that road, broad and gummy-surfaced, supported something all the time, while the ditches on both sides were used by endless lines of plodding Americans, faint from hunger and thirst, almost exhausted for want of sleep, but all thrilled by the hunger for Huns that will be satisfied only by victory and peace.

"The World was about to strike the Huns. Marshal Foch was behind us. So, these hungering Americans plodded on and on, without complaint. That road with its babel of streaming traffic told us something big was about to happen. And we all secretly congratulated ourselves on being considered good enough to have a part in the big show.

"The tanks were the most cheering sight. In our previous ventures over the top we had done for the Hun with artillery and rifles only. We never had seen a tank in action, but we believed it would be a comfort to have them with us. Had we only known!

"Toward evening it was pure agony to pass a French kitchen, located in the woods that flanked both sides of the road. We took to robbing the water-wagons as they passed. The Frenchman is a voluptuous little cusser and we gave those poor drivers every chance to display their undoubted talent. They slashed at us with their whips when their voices gave out, but we didn't mind. When a man gets to a certain stage of dryness, such as he might feel after thirty Turkish baths have fried him out, a thousand devils wouldn't prevent him from robbing a water-wagon. It reminded me of Kipling's 'But when it comes to slaughter, you'll do your work on water, and you'll kiss the bloomin' boots of him that's got it.' Good old Kip—he knows!

"Looking back along the line, I saw a lad with a loaf of French bread. I stepped aside and waited for him. In the presence of that loaf I actually trembled, as a lover will in the presence of some peach he would die to possess.

"'Where'd you get it?'

"'Frenchman—the makin's,' came between the gulps.

"Congestion soon halted the line, and I soon procured three loaves of bread and a cup of heavenly wine. They cost me half a tobacco sack (all I had) and a pack of cigarette papers. And the French cook, by a wealth of gestures and a shameful waste of words, finally informed me that the grand show would open in the morning. The bread disappeared. And all spirits in my vicinity perked up wonderfully.

"Every now and then we'd come to a place in the road where a shell had exploded recently. At one place there were five and a half horses and some blue helmets. These were dragged aside hastily. And then what a furious race ensued as the halted traffic now dashed ahead to close the gap in the stream of war wheels.

"Around 5 o'clock the Major, who had gone to headquarters in a commandeered automobile, rejoined us and we stopped for a rest. I dropped down in the ditch and eased my pack straps from the spots that ached. I forgot to state that I had been attached to battalion headquarters as liaison non-com. The Major came over and sat beside me.

"'Sergeant,' he said, 'have the men got emergency rations?' I knew my company had none.

"'No, sir,' I replied.

"'What!' he exclaimed. 'Why in h— haven't they? Maj. G—— (who had taken charge while our Major was in hospital) told me they had!'

"I could have told him why they had none, but refrained. He is the finest man in the Marine outfit. He is known as 'Johnny the Hard'. The title was bestowed by his affectionate men years ago because he will bawl any one out from a buck private in the rear rank to a Colonel on the general staff for good reason. He is as keen as a razor, indefatigable in the line of duty, a soldier from top to toes, and an old hand. I wasn't in the mood to receive a tongue lashing, so I referred him to the Captain of the nearest company. After the Major had exploded with the effect of a big gas shell we resumed the hike.

"Finally, after several parleys with French officers and a close study of maps, the Major struck out along a quieter road. We hiked and hiked and hiked till our shoes quit squeaking. Dusk dropped his curtain. The road gradually became deserted. Soon we were the only men in sight. We zigzagged from side to side, ducking trees cut off by big shells. Suddenly we were confronted by a gesticulating Frenchman, who refused to let us pass. His eloquence barred our way. The Major was impatient. He sent back for an interpreter. Then the Frenchman had an idea. He grasped the Major's arm and, pointing along the road, he dramatically uttered, 'Boche!'

" 'What!' said our Major, 'Combien kilometres?'

" 'Non, non! Kilometre!' hissed the little Man in Blue.

"One hundred metres at forty inches a metre, turned over in our minds and made us uncomfortable. As an Englishman would have said: 'If hide 'ad a 'andkerchief hide 'ave mopped me brow.' The Major shook hands admiringly with that Frenchman. And we discreetly withdrew to a woods, like a lady to her boudoir, assisted by five shells that burst on either side the road. A runner from R. H. I. found us and delivered an order to dig in.

"Meantime darkness had blotted out all but the trees, and between the bark of 'heavies' we caught the deep-throated roll of thunder. A soldier who has had two months of open work of out-door warfare, in which artillery has played the leading rôle, has to be very, very tired to ignore an order to dig in, a scant kilometre back of the first line, the worst spot on the field. We dug in. When nature's storm broke we meekly rolled up in our ponchos and dropped to the ground asleep. The closing misery of that day came in the shape of rain-water trickling down my back as sleep knocked us unconscious. And I had not strength enough left to mutter a curse!

"Before dawn next morning we were up, standing by, awaiting the barrage. We were not scheduled to work that day. But reserves are held in readiness to act instantly. The last of the tanks that had found shelter in our wood the preceding day trundled away by 4 A. M. Nothing was left to divert our attention from gnawing stomachs. We tightened our belts again and tried to concentrate on the barrage to come. We expected something extraordinary. But we were utterly unprepared for what did happen.

"At 4:30 A. M., July 18th, there was an explosion— a grand, glorious, terrific, ear-gouging explosion. It never wavered. It lasted for hours without interruption. The earth shook up and down and sideways. The very foundations of the Teutonic dynasties must have trembled fearfully, for it heralded the long-awaited new order of things. The Driver became the Driven, the Offender the Defender. I thought I knew what a barrage was. I had heard 1,600 guns of all calibres discharged simultaneously and had thought it the Himalayan topmost peak of din. But this barrage! It shook the leaves off the trees! The heavens came down and the earth went up; I can't describe it. *The great organ of eternity was rolling out its thunder from the world's end to world's end. The mills of the Gods were grinding, and they grind exceeding small.*

"And we revelled in this gargantuan explosion like starving men set down to milk and honey. Forgotten were our empty stomachs! Forgotten were parched throats, cracked lips, blistered feet, aching joints, and wet clothes! Our eyes shone like a zealot's and our hearts filled with the glory and splendour of that mighty thunder. O, man! What a grand

and glorious feeling that was! One lad said: 'I never want to have a grander feeling or I'd just naturally die of joy.'

"Two hours later, the guns still on double-forte, we started up the road on which the Frenchman had flagged us the night before. A hundred yards beyond where he had turned us back lay a dead German. Near him was a machine gun placed to command that road. This road was a replica of other roads. If anything, the congestion now was worse. Huge trees uprooted by giant shells required detours, while the engineers worked like beavers to clear away the massive tops. Reserve tanks and artillery lined either side of the road. Ambulances now mixed with the various wagons of war. Weaving in and out through the traffic came the walking wounded. Germans bearing improvised stretchers and batches of from ten to thirty Boche prisoners. The air was peopled with airplanes. The sharp clatter of their machine guns occasionally rose above the rumble of the artillery.

"We had travelled about three kilometres when we met the first big haul of the front-line fishermen. There were about 200 Huns and five officers. The boys have learned a lot about human nature in the last few months. They read faces. The face of one of those officers roused their ire. He was brazen and contemptuous. 'Kill the Boche!' some one shouted. Many a hand slipped to an automatic. Lordy, how we hate the German officer, arrogant, full of bile, and raging inwardly at his capture! One of the grimy-faced guards taking those prisoners to the rear shouted after us:

" 'We got more than this spawn! You oughta see the artillery! Some 210s.' Better news never came back from the front line.

"In our first encounters with the Boche we learned many things. We learned that the German infantry has a horror of hand-to-hand fighting and will run or surrender rather than try such combat with us. We learned that the sole protection of the Boche artillery lay in the effectiveness of front-line machine guns and its own accuracy. We came to believe the backbone of the German infantry was their artillery. Every battle since has strengthened that belief. And such a situation in any army has a demoralizing effect. The infantry should be the backbone of the artillery! Our boys say: 'Oh, if the powers-that-be would only dispense with the artillery on both sides and let us mix it man to man, we'd have Berlin in a week!' That's the spirit protecting our artillery, and it's appreciated. You may get an idea of the confidence placed by our artillerymen in our infantry when I tell you I have seen three-inch pieces drawn up within 2,000 yards of the front line, where the fighting could be seen with the naked eye and one had to duck bullets. That's coöperation with a vengeance. So news of the capture of heavy artillery, the only dependable fighting machinery of the enemy, tickled us all over and clear through. Further reports set the number of cannon captured as 200, ranging from 77s or three-inch to 210s or eight-inch. And the absence of reply to our battering batteries confirmed such reports.

"We were wild with glee. Other reports dealt with the conduct of the fleeing Germans, the demoralization following the loss of their artillery, the capture of a Boche Colonel and his staff, and the taking of fifteen villages.

"Meantime our battalion took up a position at the edge of the wood and awaited orders. After the first excitement passed our attention fell back on our empty stomachs. We counted again the hours since our last meal. It was forty-two. For that many years, it seemed, we had been without food, sleep, and water rations and we had worked as men never worked before. The nervous strain had kept us on our feet and yet those men were willing, yes fretting, to get into the thick of battle. Who kept us back in reserve? With what righteous anger the men asked that question. They declared they would bear such misery for months just to keep the Hun running.

"Then the miracle happened. A big truck drew up by the roadside and began to dump boxes—boxes of canned beef, tomatoes, prunes, and bread. Fifteen minutes later there were a thousand utterly radiant soldiers ravenously gulping a real feed and easing their thirst—with tomato juice.

"But war considers no man's pleasure. In the middle of the feast came the rattle and clatter of machine guns, temporarily acting as aerial defence. Came swooping down from the sky directly over us four planes. 'The Iron Cross!' We grabbed our rifles. 'Germans!' 'Hold on!' as rifles were sighted; 'it's a Frenchman and three Heinies after him!'

"Points in this aerial battle at close range come and go too quickly for recognition almost. The clever Gaul is outwitting the Boche pilots. The four planes whirl directly over our heads 100 feet from the ground, the Frenchman a few yards ahead and lowest. They clear the tops of the trees and circle over a field in front of us. The Boche pilots pour lead at the handicapped Frenchman, who desperately turns the nose of his craft upward. The Germans must have been looking for such a move. They elevate and close in on him. A fierce rattle of machine guns! A plane drops nose-foremost. Straight down it comes, then—we gasp in avid admiration—within twenty feet of the ground the French pilot with superb daring jerks his responsive machine to a level keel and sails off, clipping the heads off the grain!

"We shout a millionth part of the joy we feel and open fire on the Boche machines that hover, it seems angrily, over where the Gaul should have met disaster. Their amazed disappointment actually evidences itself in the way they handle their craft. They attempt several times to swoop down on the Frenchman, who has alighted. But a thousand rifles in the hands of Marines who know how to shoot is a court of death. Each time they approach we tear holes in their wings. They must have gone only for more ammunition, for we had hardly finished our meal when they returned with two companions. We took cover and opened fire. They manœuvred and swooped down on us, all together, spitting bullets by the reel. But the way we used our rifles made those Hun machine guns look pale and ill. Things began to thicken up when a French air squadron plumped into sight. Our buzzards left abruptly. We were sorry! We were having the time of our lives! And we might have got 'em all. Then we were ordered to dig in, and with full stomachs and light hearts we turned to. By 5 o'clock every one had a hole. At 5:30 we left the wood and our holes behind to take a position nearer the front line, which was pushing ahead with surprising rapidity.

"We came to a crossroads and turned to the right. From here one could see a deal of country. It was all grain fields. Streams of men, of horses and artillery were everywhere. We cut across an enormous field of wheat. On our right lay a French plane, apparently none the worse for its adventure. To the left lay a big German plane. One wondered if the little Frenchman had conquered the big Hun. To our left was also a German trench and the dead who remained after one of our tanks had passed its length.

" 'Here they come!'

"I looked ahead and saw a column of men—Germans—marching toward us, four abreast. Apparently there was no end to that column. I bethought me to count the fours. At least twenty officers were at the head of that column. They were the happiest prisoners alive, I believe. Those Germans who spoke English cheered us on. One shouted: 'Give 'em hell, boys. It won't last long!' Those who spoke French shouted encouragement to the Frenchmen and the burden of their shout was: 'Fini la guerre!' (Finish the war.) The French were tickled. I counted fours to the extent of 205 and lost track then through trying to hear everything that was said. I estimated the batch of prisoners at 1,300. And the majority were so young. It made one's heart ache to think of how recently they had been dragged from their mothers' hearths by the Kaiser's mailed fist. Nothing but rosy-cheeked, red-lipped, bright-eyed boys! We vowed again to do our best in the coming fight that the world might see a speedy end of the outrageous clique of men who send to hopeless slaughter the children of their nation for the sake of mere temporal pomp and power and to protect their own rhinoceros hides! There was pure murder in the men's eyes now.

"We passed a line of batteries, famous French 75s, pounding, pounding. Over the country ahead we counted five hangars, or what had been hangars. Now they were grotesquely twisted steel skeletons, deserted by the Huns. We passed through a wee village, came into another wheat field, formed for attack, and stopped for the night. We occupied a knoll. On the slope below was a line of queer-looking dots. In the hollow proper were three 75 batteries. Up to the left were still more batteries. We searched the landscape in the direction they were shooting. We found their target. It was on the farthest hill. The last rays of the sun outlined it clearly. It was a long line of tanks. Their artillery having been captured, the Huns brought into the fight these tanks as a substitute. When we first sighted them they were spitting fire from their one-pounders. And they were moving. In a half hour they were in ruins. And through glasses we saw the German infantry fleeing past them, running as only scared Huns can run, helter-skelter, every man for himself, the devil take the hindmost. Our batteries rested and a skirmish line of Americans came on the scene pursuing the Germans. The hill was ours!

"Then we went down to examine those queer dots below us. 'Guns, German guns. Eighty-eights. Hundred and fives!' And we tore down on them. They were placed in deep holes, with only the muzzles sticking out. Large piles of shells were near each gun. The Germans transport their shells in wicker baskets, small calibres having three compartments. The 210-shell is given its own basket.

"After the sun had set the slope before us began to be covered with Chasseurs de Cheval, the light cavalry of France. They were massed on that slope by the thousand and still they came. We wondered where they all came from and where they had obtained their horses. Again we had that feeling of doing big things. For they were to go over the top with us on the morrow.

"The day was succeeded by one of those nights

that sets a fellow to dreaming of the folks back home.
I had the 10-to-12 watch. From the road at the
right came the steady clinkety-clank, clinkety-clank
of tanks—an endless stream of tanks going forward for the morning attack. I had not dreamed
there were so many tanks in the whole of France
or in the world. To the right and left and in front
the Germans sent up star-shells that lighted the
country in an unearthly glare. One could judge
the extent of their demoralization by the continuous
stream of star-shells they sent up. Often a cannon
would bark somewhere. Always it was our cannon.
The Huns had none. How safe we felt with their
guns harvested behind our lines. When 12 o'clock
came I rolled up in my wet blanket and slept as I
never slept before behind the front line in easy reach
of the Germans. So ended the morning and the
evening of the first day."

"Base Hospital No. 20, A. E. F.

"Dear Brownie—I'm a very lucky hombre. Went
over the top at 8:20 A. M., July 21st. High explosive
shell hit the road alongside of me and never touched
me. The gas blinded and choked me and I fell
into a shallow dugout alongside the road. Just then
the dugout was blown up and the last of my sensations was of floating up, up, up, minus my left leg.
Some time later, when I got back to earth, a hospital apprentice assured me I was all there. Considering all this I'm feeling pretty good.

"I've been to the land from which only cooks and

chaplains return. And I've all my arms and legs!
Why? I don't know, unless God and Our Country
has further use for me before the Kaiser puts my
address on a shell. An English Tommy told me
before I went up to the battlefront that if I were
lucky my trials and troubles would end the first day
and were I extremely out of luck, I'd duck along
for a year or two. I smiled incredulously then.
But he was right. I believe that if it ever is necessary for me again to endure what the last seventeen
days have battered in and out of me, I should be
a raving maniac. Nothing in history, in heaven or
earth, nor nightmares of a deranged mind can offer
simile to this war. Sherman's expression is of the
far past, and civilized. At that time it may have
been an apt description. But we have the electric
furnace to-day, with its thousand degrees of heat.
Compare it with a candle. So battles have intensified, until they are a million hells rolled into one.
This is weak, weak! For no man, though he command
all the knowledge of the ages and the universe, could
in a terse expression conjure for the world an adequate description or comparison of war to-day. But
I'm not going to continue in that strain.

"I've had a few days' rest since my last battle
and my nerves have quieted considerably here in the
hospital. Oh, the sweet rest! After one has survived
nine days of continuous shell fire, witnessed all the
numbing scenes of the most hellish bombardments
by shells of from 1- to 15-inch calibre, classed shrapnel, high explosives, and gas, one may be excused for

a slight case of nerves. Considering that we had neither dugouts nor trenches for protection, that we held fast under what veteran French officers swore was one of the most terrific shell-storms in their vast experience, that we actually stopped the Germans and drove the arrogant Huns back—considering all this we Marines, every one of us, believe ourselves the luckiest warriors in the world. But let us digress.

"It has ceased raining at last and France appears to be doing her utmost to square herself on the 'sunny stuff.' Man, this is a fine morning, the sun shining brightly, the wind blowing gently over a rolling green country stretching away to the uttermost reach of sight, dotted here and there with clumps of wood and red-tiled, picturesque stone houses. It's a beautiful part of a wonderful country, but for all of its promising beauty there is something lacking. Even a novice can sense the air of desertion and desolation hanging over the placid scene. It affects one like the painting of an artist who cannot reproduce the life, the soul of his subject. Life! There's not a living creature to be seen. No moving thing in all those miles of country. No haze of smoke haloing yonder village, no cattle browsing on those verdant slopes, no farmers working back and forth across those strips of cultivated ground. The soul of the country has been stunned, battered into unconsciousness by the ravaging Hun.

"A closer scrutiny of the nearer buildings brings a sense of the grotesque—they don't look plumb;

they're out of true. It's too far away to be distinct, but the perpendicular line of yonder steeple curves in and out again as though some giant hand had torn away a fistful of the masonry. The roof of the house off to the right appears to sag in the centre and there stands a wall perhaps thirty feet in height, without a supporting side—What's that? A dull, droning humming sound like a monstrous bee overhead. There's another, louder, nearer! 'Putt, putt-t, prrrrrht—putt.'—Machine guns! There they are, outlined against the sun, two transparent yellow spots that circle, whirl, dive and mount swiftly, gracefully, the poetry of motion, manœuvring for mastery, majestic in their elemental swoop and dash and bravery. Two lone eagle-men in the eagle's realm are in combat. They charge. They feint. They tack and twist. They dive and bounce upward, wings flashing, like giant ospreys or cormorants, love-rivals. Thrilling, thrilling, thrilling! As you watch them, your heart in your bosom seems to move in concert with every swoop and dash of the eagle-men. The result of this battle, in a day or two, may mean life or death to us who walk terra firma.

"There, a black ball of smoke opens beneath those dashing fliers. Another and another. High explosive. Now two balls of yellow smoke, closer to them than the black—shrapnel. Ah, one is falling. One eagle tumbles like a plummet. The round world rises to meet him. He's afire! French or Boche? We don't know, but we hope——

"Wommph—Bzzzzhhhr—Bang! A 155-shell has come.

"The face of the earth is deserted. Not a man is in sight where a moment before were twenty. Vanished! Where? Were they blown to atoms? See those little mounds of earth, neatly covered, carefully concealed by boughs and leaves? Beside each of those mounds is a hole and in each hole a man, maybe two. While you listened to the song of the enemy shell, they dropped into the bowels of the earth.

"At first we lost men through inexperience. They couldn't tell a shell's direction by its whistle. Some of us ducked when there was no need. Some of us did not duck when the need was imperative. But now our ears are educated and we can spend more time than formerly outside our dugouts. We do not needlessly tire ourselves climbing in and out.

"Our invincible sense of humour sticks with us Americans. That is the miracle amid all this blood and death and crashing of cannon. And it is worked overtime. Everything in this battle life is so novel and grotesque. Passing through a trench I came on a gunnery Sergeant sitting in his dugout, the roof of which had been blown off. He was squeezing the stump of his arm, which had been amputated near the shoulder by a piece of high-explosive shell. At the instant I stopped to give aid there ran down on us a panic-stricken youth who had been rudely ejected from his hole by a 155. In passing us he stumbled over the Sergeant's detached arm in the centre of the ditch. He paused for a second, glanced at what had interrupted his speed, raised his eyes to the Sergeant's stump, moaned dolefully, and resumed his flight at redoubled speed. The wounded Sergeant spat out a copious spout of tobacco-juice and, with twinkling eyes, remarked: 'Reminds me of the first time I had to drown a batch of kittens.'

"I've seen men laugh at the antics of their comrades whose eyes and mouths had been filled with the dirt and corruption a Maxim machine gun tore up. I was crouched in the entrance of a dugout during one of the Germans' famous barrages when a lad jumped out of the ditch and in front of me. At that moment three 155-shells fell and burst within a 15-foot radius. The terrific explosion hurled the boy straight back into the dugout and his feet hit me squarely in the face. When I recovered my wits I called out, inquiring if he were hurt. He chuckled and said 'H—, no.'

"During that same barrage two men previously posted fifty yards ahead of the line with an automatic were forgotten in the excitement, but they stuck to their post. Some one happened to think of them about half an hour after the show started and I ducked out to get them in. I had little hope of finding them alive. I ran out into the wheat field in their direction when I heard a shell coming. I flattened out on the ground. The top of my head floated in a crazy, gyrating course toward heaven, then snapped back into position. The shell had exploded ten feet on my right. One of the lads of my quest was long and rangy and hailed from Texas; the other, short and stubby, was from Georgia.

" 'She cut 'em both off,' came the Texan's voice out of darkness on my right.

" 'Th' 'ell she did?' said Shorty.

" 'Shorty, I reckon we'd better drag this huzzy outa here.'

" 'Them's my sentiments,' Shorty agreed.

"We all returned together. The shell had lit, or alighted, under the tripod of their automatic rifle and neatly amputated both its metal legs.

"Before we went over the top a tale was told to illustrate the density of the German barrage. A Corporal walked into a first-aid post with a badly fractured arm and spoke of the terrific shelling his unit was undergoing. There being no laceration of his flesh, the puzzled doctor inquired how the Corporal had been injured.

" 'Oh, that,' said the lad; 'you see I was standing beside the hole of my dugout, leaning up against that barrage, when it suddenly lifted, letting me fall into a hole, where I lit on my arm.'

"We captured a German Lieutenant Colonel soon after our barrage lifted the first 100 yards, who thought the efficiency and speed of our artillery was due to machine work. As he surrendered he fixed his captor with a vacuous stare and said: 'Where is it—that terrible machine gun you have that shoots 75s?'

"One lad remarked: 'Rifle fire is a sweet, sweet lullaby, machine guns impress one as the humming of bees, Austrian 88s make a lot of noise that won't affect a dugout, but the lazy boys launched away back of Berlin sure disrupt the company.' And when those 8- to 15-inch shells, 'sea-bags,' we call 'em, that the French turn loose from Somewhere in France, come sailing over our heads, slow and easy, like they're just aching and fixing to drop in the centre of a German column, you should see the boys look at each other and smile!

"One will hear a 'Whispering Willie' shoved off in our direction. The boys will duck as it looses a diabolical shriek above their heads. Every ear strains to catch the explosion—nothing but a dull thud when it hits the earth. Immediately some one says, ' 'Nother dud.' We've kept track when the fire was not too heavy and found that an average of two out of every five small-calibre German shells were duds, while the larger ones average one out of five.

"One platoon in reserve was taken up on a newly established line to eliminate a pestiferous machine gun nest. After satisfactorily completing the job they returned to their dugouts to find during their absence that Fritz had tried to blow up their homes with some 205s. The last men filing into the trench were spied by enemy observers, who signalled to a battery of 88s that proceeded to accelerate the boys' movements about 100 per cent. Each man dived for his little old hole in the ground and all were safely ensconced in a twinkling, except one lad, who was seen to jump away from his hole with a terrified expression on his face and dive in with a neighbour. Whereupon an altercation—

" 'Hey, get out! There's two in here now.'

" 'Well, shove together. I'm comin' in. Can't get in mine.'

" 'Why can't you?'

" 'There's a 205-dud went through the roof and its nose is sticking out of the door.'

"Fine argument. Our respect is enormous for a dud of those dimensions. And not one of us is so heartless as to force a friend into a hole with such a cold companion. For an 8-inch shell's intentions are so indefinite.

"I really believe that the recklessness of the United States Marines saved many of our lives, astounding the enemy, hypnotizing them into forgetting their guns. And it would take incredible recklessness to counter German discipline. One Lieutenant whom I accompanied took two platoons from reserve, where they had been under continuous shell fire for seventy-two hours, to clear a wood of enemy machine guns and establish liaison on the left flank of the battalion. Advancing some 600 yards they found themselves free of the shelled area, only to be spied by a couple of Maxim machine gunners, who lost no time in announcing their presence. 'Peeung—peeung—pee-ung,' the bullets came whistling through the brush. One hit a lad on the cheek, whereupon he heaved a sigh and said: 'What a relief!' We halted the men and reconnoitred. To reach the wood sheltering the Boche we had to cross a ploughed field. The

Lieutenant took fifteen men. I followed with fifteen more and was followed in turn by another Sergeant and as many men. Each step we took was the expected last. I was sweating like a harvest hand on the Fourth, while my teeth chattered like dice in a box. Never a shot! We formed a skirmish line the shape of an L as we entered the woods, not knowing the position of any German. The word was passed to 'down' and wait for 'patrol.' As the last man on the right flank downed hell broke loose fifty feet in front of us. A machine gun in the centre and one on either flank tore up the ground, sawed off the brush, cut down saplings in front of us, and literally slapped the whole mess in our faces. The man on the right flank had failed to get down quickly enough. He's there yet.

"I was behind a three-cornered piece of rock that seemed to grow amazingly smaller each moment, and for five minutes I neither could see, hear, nor smell. Suddenly those guns ceased and, spitting the dirt out of our mouths, we took a turn at shooting, and I think our forty rifles and two 'shau-shauds' outdid the machine guns for speed and noise. But the precarious position we held, practically a wedge driven into the German line, offset the deadliest fire, for we could be surrounded in a twinkling. Back of us lay the ploughed field, devoid of cover, that had been crossed in our advance. In front and on the right and left were the enemy machine guns. 'Cannon to the right of them,' etc., popped into my mind.

"Came one of those lulls in the fire and a long line of breaking twigs, stumblings, mumblings, and sibilant commands marked the advance of the Boche. We all thought our lives had just about been lived. There was left a choice between two distasteful dilemmas: Stay where we were and become prisoners or retrace our steps across the ploughed field and become dead men. It was one or the other, pronto! And there wasn't a doubt in our minds as to which it would be. Turning your back on a line of Boche machine guns, walking away from them at midday over a ploughed field covered by their cross-fire isn't the pleasantest thing to contemplate and it is well we had little time for thinking. When word came to fall back every one was ready, believe me. No matter how long you have lived previous to such an experience you cannot know until then what a pliable and sensitive thing your backbone is. There was nothing lagging or pernickety about the step of that retreat. If we were uneasy when advancing over that field, ignorant of the German line, imagine our emotions now. Needless to say, the last few yards were covered in nothing flat. And the Germans never fired a shot.

"But they followed us and attempted to pull the same trick again. With cries of 'Help, Help,' and 'Kamerad' six men and an officer came across that field and, while they parleyed, we continued to throw up a parapet. On their part they were covering two machine guns that attempted to flank us. We held our fire while the Lieutenants shouted to each other. When the Boche officer thought his machine gun crews had had sufficient time to accomplish their task, two of the gang, who were trying to 'surrender,' dashed forward and threw hand grenades. Meantime we had obtained reinforcements and two machine guns. So the two who threw the hand grenades we used as parapets. The other five of the 'kamerad' gang will prevaricate no more. And the eight who worked with the Maxim have doubtless been reported missing in German casualty lists. I know they were missing a miscellaneous assortment of organs necessary to the functioning of the human body. For the effects of a C. E. grenade are splendid and terrible.

"Later a whole battalion attempted to take those woods without the assistance of our artillery. The enemy, with no other object than a reckless determination to foil us, ignoring his own infantry, turned a barrage into his own front line that accounted for more Boches than we did. After our objective was gained, rifles were laid by for picks and shovels. The companies reported. Those reports will be whispered into the ears of grandchildren by old, old grandmothers, whose eyes will mirror the supreme sacrifice. Such things make the chins of strong men quiver. Anyhow, it was considered best to fall back to original position. (The next morning, following a barrage, we took the wood.)

"One lad, on an isolated post, failing to get the word, was industriously entrenching himself when the Germans counter-attacked and he found himself alone, surrounded by what seemed 1,000 Boches. He reached for his rifle. He found its stock shattered by a piece of shell. A young Boche Lieutenant confronted him. There was nothing to do but surrender. He signified his helplessness. But the Germans didn't appear anxious to molest him. The Lieutenant began to jabber at Sammy, who couldn't get his drift. Several non-coms. took up the one-sided talk, when the officer gave up and Sammy got disgusted. 'H—,' says he, 'if you don't want me, I'm going back.' So saying he swung the shovel over his shoulder and boldly marched back. To his surprise and discomfiture the German Lieutenant, nodding and smiling, immediately fell in behind, followed in single file by his men.

"Suddenly it dawned upon Sammy that the Germans wished to become prisoners. The fire of conquest ran through his veins. He stopped and counted them. Fifty-nine and an officer! Oh, boy, what a haul! With a lilting step, head up, shoulders squared and chest thrown out, he peacocked back to our lines and ran smack into company headquarters, the shovel still on his shoulder. When his comrades spied those Huns, most of 'em armed and equipped, there was a sharp intake of breath, a spontaneous, unanimous 'What the h—l,' followed by a riotous grabbing of rifles. The alert Germans averted a massacre by promptly sticking up their mitts while Sammy explained. Then he was given a firearm and permitted to lead his sixty prisoners triumphantly to the rear.

"One lad from the West was tickled by the comparison we offered to a prairie dog village. He said you could sometimes slip up close enough to one of these villages to catch a glimpse of hundreds of animals sitting or frolicking around near their holes, but the moment you were sighted they were gone, each into his own hole. Their disappearance is so sudden that it makes you rub your eyes and pinch yourself. We differ from a prairie dog in that a shell never slips up on us. When five minutes pass without producing a shell several heads will be poked cautiously from the earth in a place apparently deserted. After a sniff for gas there ensues a grunting and heaving, plentifully seasoned with invectives directed at Fritz, the Kaiser, the general staff, most anything German, and the more courageous are out of their dugouts. They dig the 'monkey meat' (South American canned beef) and bread from under the debris and earth deposited by the 'Whispering Willies.'

"Those who have discretion, not valour, appear intermittently and by the time the rations have been recovered and rejuvenated every one is on the job. The meal is begun and carried along with astonishing rapidity until 'womph—bzzzzwhrrr—chapowie!' From the 'wommmph' to the 'owie' is a matter of seconds, from the men to their dugouts is a matter of feet and inches, but the most agile prairie dog could not pull the vanishing stunt better than we. For that shell has not shrieked the last 'z' before the face of the earth is deserted. Such speed would make 'Smoky' Joe bat his eyes. All the time a man is out of his hole he knows instinctively the exact direction of and distance to the entrance of his dugout. No matter how far he wanders or turns and twists, the time consumed between the report of a gun and his arrival in that dugout is invariably the same as if he had been standing by the entrance when the shell shoved off. But despite this ducking and dodging there are no troops more feared and respected by the Boche than the Marines. And we so impressed them they honoured us with the nickname 'Devil Dogs.' We are proud of it.

"The first time our battalion went over the top the leading wave entered the woods without seeing a German. About 100 yards in the woods they sighted the Boche. With a blood-freezing war-whoop they charged. Nothing on earth but concentrated cross-fire by cool machine gunners could have stopped them. And the imperial German nerve, being nothing to brag of in the first place, had been worn ragged by our artillery. That war-whoop was the straw that broke their nerve. Two crews stood by their guns. The other Germans ran. They didn't seem to care about direction. Some ran into our bayonets, some ran away from them, some didn't have nerve enough to haul themselves free of their dugouts. But it made no difference. The result was the same. They're there yet. One German Captain jumped up from his dugout, wild-eyed and dishevelled.

" 'What in Gott's name is it?' he shouted in good English. 'Are these devils we face drunk or bloodthirsty savages?' Then he threw a hand grenade pointblank at a Lieutenant. The 'loot' ducked and levelled his automatic at the same time, so the Captain's question is still unanswered."

After Soissons the Marines were again withdrawn to a rest area. Their casualties had been heavy and there was much reorganizing to be done and many replacement men to be trained and fused into the brigade. By September, however, they were ready again for battle.

On September 12th Pershing started his now famous drive to reduce the St. Mihiel salient, and the Marine Brigade, with General Lejeune at its head, was again called upon. The Second Division, now rated as first-class shock troops, were given a place of honour in the hardest fighting along the southern side of the salient, where the German resistance was stiffest. They smashed through that stubborn line in record time.

Here is the story of that operation as gleaned from the Pershing and Daniels reports: On August 30th a large section of the St. Mihiel front was turned over to General Pershing. Our Second Division was placed in the First Army Corps, with the Fifth, 82nd, and 90th Divisions, under Major General Hunter Liggett. On September 11th the Second Division took over the line running from Remenauville to Limey. On September 12th the First Corps, with three divisions of the Third Corps, began an advance which continued irresistibly until the salient was wiped out.

On the night of the 14th and the morning of the 15th the Second Division attacked with two days' objectives laid out for them. They crossed the Rupt de Mad and occupied Thiaucourt, the first day's objective. But it never occurred to them to stop there. They scaled the heights beyond Thiaucourt and pushed forward to a line running from the Zammes-Joulney Ridge to Binvaux Forest, reaching their second day's objective at 2:50 P. M. of the first day. This extraordinary accomplishment was not achieved without sacrifice. The division's casualties numbered 1,000, of whom 134 were killed, but they captured eighty German officers, 3,200 men, ninety-odd cannon, and vast stores, besides slaying their thousands.

The Marines were again withdrawn, to reappear on October 2nd where least expected—in the Champagne with General Gouraud's Fourth Army, which drove north to free the Rheims from the German clutch. In the region of Somme-Py they attacked like a whirlwind and broke through the German line for a gain of six kilometres, leading all other troops in the attack. They seized the German second line positions in front of them, capturing the armoured trenches and wired lines. On the second day, October 3rd, they were ready for the main attack on Blanc Mont and in the face of a devastating machine gun fire they assisted in the capture of that stronghold, which was accomplished with such amazing speed that the Boches were swept off their feet.

The story of the Second Division's part in that

operation is thus succinctly told in General Pershing's report: "On October 2 to 9 our Second and 36th Divisions were sent to assist the French in an important attack against the old German positions before Rheims. The Second conquered the complicated defence works on their front against a persistent defence worthy of the grimmest period of trench warfare and attacked the strongly held wooded hill of Blanc Mont, which they captured in a second assault, sweeping over it with consummate dash and skill. This division then repulsed strong counterattacks before the village and cemetery of Ste. Etienne and took the town, forcing the Germans to fall back from before Rheims and yield positions they had held since September, 1914." On October 9th the Second Division was relieved by the 36th, having done its part in breaking the Hun's tenacious hold on the hills of Champagne and at last setting free the martyred cathedral city.

The story of that action is told thus by Edwin L. James, correspondent of the *New York Times:*

"It is now permitted to give a comprehensive sketch of the rôle played by the Americans in the brilliant Champagne advance of General Gouraud's army.

"This story is one of the most absorbingly interesting of the Americans at war, not only because of the glorious work of our 'veteran' 2nd Division, but because of the remarkably effective work done by the 36th Division, from Texas, which, never having been under shell fire and not even entirely organized, jumped into the bitter battle and made gains that were sensational. Never having heard the scream of shells before, they fought day after day under terrific shell fire, and went after the Germans in true ranger style. An official order of the French General calls this one of the brilliant performances of the war.

"America knows well the bright record of the 2nd Division of Infantry, the regiments of which there are the 5th and 6th Marines and the 9th and 23rd Infantry. These are the boys who stopped the Germans up in Belleau Wood, back in June when the foe thought he was going to Paris.

"This division played a good rôle in the St. Mihiel battle. It went into line on the evening of October 2, taking over a position of three and a half kilometres running westward from Somme-Py. To get a good jumping-off place for the attack to begin the next morning, they seized the German second line positions in front of them, taking armoured trenches and wired lines. When the main attack started on October 3, at 5:30 o'clock in the morning, the Americans were successful from the start.

"Raked from a German position on their left flank, known as the 'Essen Trench,' from which enfilading machine guns swept the advancing ranks, the divisions sent part of a regiment out of its sector to take the trench. So fast was the pace of these men that they reached the German observatory of Blanc Mont before the foe knew what had happened, an observer there being captured while writing out a report that the German counter-attack was going well.

"On October 3, the 2nd Division made an advance of about six kilometres. The men got so far ahead of the troops on the left that they were in danger of being encircled when a fresh French division was put in behind them to protect their left flank. Next morning they resumed the attack at 4:30. They ran into very heavy

German machine gun and artillery resistance north of the Arnes River, but reached Ste. Etienne.

"The day of the 5th was devoted to consolidating the newly won positions. All the time there was a murderous fire from the Germans. The American positions had to be held under front and flank fire until the troops on the left and right got up. Meanwhile the advance of the Americans and the taking of Blanc Mont had decided the Germans to make a withdrawal from the Rheims salient, the execution of which greatly bettered our positions.

"On October 6, two regiments of Marines, which had been in the heaviest fighting, were relieved by a brigade of the 36th Division, never under fire before. After short artillery preparation, the attack was renewed October 8, at the same time that the Germans delivered a heavy counter-attack on the right of the division front. This was repulsed after bitter fighting.

"The next day was devoted to consolidation, while on October 10 the second brigade of the 36th relieved the 9th and 23rd Regiments of the 2nd Division, completing the relief.

"From that time on our part in the advance was effected by these young Texans, entirely new to war. On October 11 they forced the Germans back, occupying Machault and Semide, and on the next day, against heavy machine-gun resistance, reached the banks of the Aisne."

On October 17th General Gaulin, commanding the corps in which the Second and 36th Divisions served in this fighting, issued this general order:

"On October 2 the 2nd American Division, having arrived during the night on the sector of the 21st Army Corps, attacked the fortified crest of Blanc Mont, captured it in a few hours in spite of the desperate resistance of the enemy, and in the following days made an extended advance on the slopes to the north for the purpose of consolidating his victory. The 36th American Division, of recent formation, and as yet incompletely organized, was ordered on the night of October 6 and 7 to relieve, under conditions particularly delicate, the 2nd American Division and dislodge the enemy from the crests north of St. Etienne and the Arnes, and throw him back to the Aisne.

"Although being under fire for the first time, the young soldiers of General Smith, rivalling in their combative spirit and tenacity the old and valiant regiments of General Lejeune, have accomplished their mission in its entirety. All may be proud of the task they accomplished. To all the General commanding the army corps is happy to address the most cordial expression of his recognition and his best wishes for their future service. The past is proof of the future.

"GAULIN."

And here is General Lejeune's order, in which the pride of the Marine is manifest:

France,

Oct. 11, 1918.

"OFFICERS AND MEN OF THE 2ND DIVISION:

"It is beyond my power of expression to describe fitly my admiration for your heroism. You attacked magnificently and you seized Blanc Mont Ridge, the keystone of the arch constituting the enemy's main position. You advanced beyond the ridge, breaking the enemy's lines, and you held the ground gained with a tenacity which is unsurpassed in the annals of war.

"As a direct result of your victory, the German armies

east and west of Rheims are in full retreat, and by drawing on yourselves several German divisions from other parts of the front you greatly assisted the victorious advance of the allied armies between Cambrai and St. Quentin.

"Your heroism and the heroism of our comrades who died on the battlefield will live in history forever, and will be emulated by the young men of our country for generations to come.

"To be able to say when this war is finished, 'I belonged to the 2nd Division; I fought with it at the battle of Blanc Mont Ridge,' will be the highest honour that can come to any man.

"JOHN A. LEJEUNE,

"Major General, United States Marine Corps, Commanding."

Finally, on November 1st, General Pershing started the drive which proved to be the last great struggle of the war. It was that mighty sweep toward Sedan, that reaching for the very heart of the Hun.

The Germans massed their best troops and a tremendous artillery support and opposed every step of the advance with the utmost bitterness. It was a fight to the death. An interminable line of murderous German machine guns, but a few feet apart, was thrown across the line of the American advance. The casualties were terrific.

For two weeks the Germans succeeded in beating back the most determined American attacks in front of Landres and St. Georges. Then the battling Second Division was hurled in. Operating at the

centre, they started an irresistible push on the very
afternoon that the Germans began to show signs of
weakening and pressed forward until they controlled
the heights below Beaumont. They broke through
that living fortress for five kilometres the first day,
leading all other divisions, and for the first time
since the beginning of the war the official German
communiqué admitted that the line had been pierced.

This advance made possible the shelling of the
vital Mezieres-Metz railway. The advance became
a pursuit, with the Germans on the run and the
Second Division ever in the van. Forty kilometres
were covered in seven days, German soldiers surrendered in companies, and the end of the war was
in sight.

The soldier does not like to dwell on casualties,
but the casualty list is often the best indication of
the character of the fighting. Certainly the path
which the Marines trod in France was no easy one.
Of the various figures that have been given out,
those offered by General Barnett in his annual report are the most reliable, though still subject to
revision. In all, 21,323 enlisted men of the Marine
Corps and 540 officers were sent to France. Between April 1 and September 1, 1918, the casualties
amounted to 23 per cent. of the gross strength,
though many of the units saw no action. During
that period 44 officers and 1,116 enlisted men were
killed and 76 officers and 2,832 men severely wounded. Only 25 Marines remained prisoner in the
hands of the Germans on September 1st. Surren-

dering wasn't popular at the time and the only way to capture a Marine was to knock him senseless first. After September 1st took place the bloody fighting in the St. Mihiel, Rheims, and Sedan regions, increasing the casualty list and the percentage materially; authentic figures are not available at the time of writing. I have seen it estimated that of the 8,000 who had some part in the action about Belleau Wood, 6,200 were at least hit by a bullet or fragment of shell, and that half of the men and officers in the fighting brigade who were not killed were at one time or another knocked out of action. The Marines won glory in France, but they paid a terrible price.

The story of the Marines in France is told. Our brave brigade had gone in at one of the darkest moments of the war and had seen the thing through till sunshine pierced the clouds. They saw the tide of battle turn there on the Marne at Château-Thierry. They saw Marshal Foch prove to all the world that German armies could be defeated and the German line broken. They saw him assume the offensive, and they joined him in the last grim push to victory.

And so, as I write these lines, the dream of the Marines is coming true—to follow the retreating Hun across the Rhine, for they have been chosen to march side by side with the honour divisions of the Allied armies in the forefront of the peace-compelling Army of Occupation. Long live the United States Marines!

PART III

SOLDIERS OF THE SEA

CHAPTER XIV

The Story of the Marine Corps

THE exploit of the United States Marines at Belleau Wood now forms a glowing page in history which all the world may read, but back of it lies a history, less spectacular perhaps, but world-embracing in its scope and honourable among military and naval annals. "From the halls of Montezuma to the shores of Tripoli," from Cuba to the Behring Sea, from Veru Cruz to Peking the Marines have stood for over a century as the strong arm of the United States Government, the embodiment of the American spirit of justice, order, and fair dealing. That history of a hundred daring deeds well done forms a tradition which lies at the bottom of our wonderful *esprit de corps*.

The American Marines were first organized by resolution of the Continental Congress on November 10, 1775. They served in the Revolution, the war with Tripoli, the War of 1812, the Mexican War, the Civil War, and a hundred affairs of less importance. The volume of that history has become part and parcel of the traditions of the Corps, but since dates and terse statements of action make but dull reading, I will spare my readers the boredom of delving deeper into the past than the Spanish War.

But before I begin the story of the Marines as I myself have known them, I beg leave to quote from an article on "Sea Soldiers" which appeared in the *New York Tribune* of October 13, 1916.

"Considering the part it has played in the world's history of warfare, there is no fighting unit less understood, less appreciated, or even less known than the Marines. Having taken his share in the making and obliterating of maps since the days of the Phœnician galleys and the biremes of the Grecian maritime states, at least five centuries before the Christian Era, down to the present day, the chroniclers of the glories of arms of all civilized peoples have mentioned the Marine in many a stirring passage. And yet, to-day, a very large part of the population of maritime nations, and certainly of the United States, do not know what a Marine really is.

"The Marines have proved their patriotism and devotion to our country for over a hundred years. Throughout this period they have been in the front rank of America's defenders. They have been zealous participants in nearly every expedition and action in which the Navy has been engaged. In many trying campaigns with their brethren of the Army they have won distinction. The globe has been their stage.

"They have fought at Tripoli, in Mexico, and the Fiji Islands. They were on the job in Paraguay, at Harper's Ferry, at Kisembo, on the West Coast of Africa, and in Panama. They fought the Japanese at Shimonoseki, the savages in Formosa, and the forts in Korea. They suppressed seal poaching in the Behring Sea and protected the lives and property of American citizens in Honolulu, Chili, and China. These and many more things have the United States Marines accomplished.

"The Navy has in the Marine Corps a little army of its own, which, without causing international complications, without disturbing stock markets, and without even attracting undue attention, it may pick up and move to some disturbed centre in a foreign land for the protection of American lives and property. These Soldiers of the Sea move speedily and unostentatiously, frequently nipping a revolution in the bud before the world at large knows that there has really been any cause for concern.

"They are the first men on the ground in case of trouble with a foreign power and the first men in battle in case of hostilities. Great mobility and facilities for quick action are required of the Marines. They are kept in readiness to move at a moment's notice. In many of the actions in which they have been engaged they have had to contend against great odds in the way of superior numbers.

"Aldridge says: 'Before a single vessel of the Navy went to sea, a corps was organized, and a detachment of it won, on the Island of New Providence—one of the Bahamas—early in 1777, the first fight in the history of the regular Navy. In this noteworthy engagement the attacking party, consisting of 300 Marines and landsmen, under Major Nichols, captured the forts and other defences of the enemy after a struggle of a few hours, and secured a quantity of stores and British cannon.'"

So much for ancient history and a running start. After my own appointment in 1892, up to the time of the Spanish War, the Marines were engaged in only minor activities, such as protection service in Honolulu, China, and Korea. In none of these affairs did I personally have any part.

At the time of the outbreak of the Spanish War, I had been detailed for service aboard ship, and it so happened that, as First Lieutenant, I was in command of the Marines on the battleship *Maine* when she was blown up and sunk in Havana Harbour in February, 1898. It was a Marine, one Private Anthony, then serving as Captain's orderly, who came quietly aft to the Captain's cabin after the explosion with the historic remark, "I have to report, Captain, that the ship is sinking."

I was transferred to Key West and remained there through March, during the meetings of the Board of Inquiry. Then I returned to New York. War was declared in April and I was shortly afterward ordered out on active service with the fleet. The American liner *St. Louis* steamed into New York Harbour on a Saturday night and was promptly converted into an auxiliary cruiser of the United States Navy. Supplies, ammunition, and four six-pound guns were rushed aboard, Captain Goodrich and Ensign Payne of the Navy being placed in charge of the ship's crew. They were the only naval men aboard. I embarked on Sunday with a Marine guard of forty-five men, the only enlisted men aboard, and on Monday we sailed. We mounted the six-pounders at sea, two forward and two aft.

For two weeks we patrolled the sea east of the Windward Islands in search of Cervera's fleet, which, the reports stated, had left Spain. As ill luck would have it we never saw that fleet. We reported on the appointed day at Guadeloupe and then went on to St. Thomas. On the day after we left those waters Cervera went through.

Seagrave, the first officer of the ship, who had been in the English cable service, told Captain Goodrich that he knew the location of all the submarine cables and stated that the cable running to San Juan could easily be picked up. The Captain decided to cut the cable and we steamed out about ten miles from San Juan. We had no grapnels aboard, so one was made in the fire room. We picked up the cable and finished the job in about half an hour. Then we joined the fleet that had been bombarding San Juan.

When Captain Goodrich reported to Admiral Sampson regarding the cables, we were ordered to proceed to Santiago and there cut the cable running to Kingston, Jamaica. This was not such an easy task, for the job had to be done under the Spanish guns of Moro Castle. The tug *Wompatuck* was ordered to accompany the *St. Louis*.

On May 18th the *St. Louis* dropped her grapnels and picked up the cable about a mile from Moro Castle. About the time we hooked the cable some old six-inch guns east of the fort opened fire on us and also some mortar batteries on the little island of Smith Cay. We had just the two six-pounders on the side toward the fort, and we returned fire with those, manning the guns with crews of Marines. I fired the gun aft while Ensign Payne had the forward gun. We silenced the old six-inch guns, but the mortars were too far away for our six-pounders.

We lay there for forty-five minutes, laboriously reeling in the cable on an anchor winch, while shells fell all around us. But, though the big *St. Louis* offered an easy target, not a shell hit us, owing, I suppose, to the notoriously bad marksmanship of the Spanish gunners. Still, it was a warm situation while it lasted.

I have sometimes been asked how it feels to be under fire, and I can only answer that it all depends on what you are doing. There have been times when I have been obliged to wait inactive for orders, with little to think about but the enemy's fire, and on such occasions I must confess that I have grown uncomfortably nervous. But there in Santiago Harbour, a fair target for the mortar batteries and the guns of the fort, with the air thick with peril, I was so intent on getting a difficult and important job done that the thought of personal danger never entered my head. Only when we turned to get away and the tension was over did anything resembling fear hasten our flight.

After that we left for Guantanamo and sent the tug in to cut the cable there. That happened to be just the day before Cervera steamed into Santiago Bay; we had missed him again. A Spanish gunboat lurking behind the point—the *Sandoval*—came out and opened fire on the tug with her three-inch Krupp. The little three-pounder on the tug could not reach her, and she was pouring in a shower of shells. So Captain Goodrich was obliged to recall the *Wompatuck* before the cable could be cut. Later on the Spaniards were obliged to sink the *Sandoval* in Guantanamo Bay.

At Santiago, again, on July 3rd, Marines served the secondary batteries, and were given credit for inflicting more damage on the enemy than the larger guns of the cruisers.

The first American troops to set foot on Cuban soil after war had been declared were Marines, and I only regret that I cannot give an eye-witness account of their remarkable exploit. It was necessary to establish at once a naval base on the shores of Cuba, and the Bay of Guantanamo was selected for this purpose—a splendid harbour where American war ships have made their home ever since. A battalion of Marines—about 400 men under Colonel Huntington—was landed on June 10, 1898, at 2 P. M. They engaged about 3,000 Spaniards, drove them inland, and, under the protection of the guns of the ships, established and held a base on the point at the entrance of the bay.

This base, however, was not secure from attack. Spanish troops, estimated at 6,000, lined the shores of the bay and the Marines were exposed to their fire. It appeared necessary to drive out the Spaniards at least from the side of the bay on which the base had been established, and they were protected by a cover of wooded hills.

Colonel Huntington learned from his scouts that the only water supply of the Spaniards on that side of the bay was what was known as Cusco Well, which was located about two miles inland from the point, and a small detachment under Colonel (now General) Elliot was detailed to go in against superior numbers and capture Cusco Well.

It was a difficult task, but the Marines lost no time in engaging the Spaniards. They had to cross hills and ravines and there were a hundred spots where large numbers of the enemy might be lying in ambush. Progress, not to be foolhardy, was necessarily slow.

The *Marblehead* had taken up a position in the harbour to assist the landed troops by shelling the well or the enemy's main position when it could be located, but at first they had no means of knowing what to shoot at.

It was then that Sergeant Major John Quick, who was afterward with me in France, pulled off the stunt that won him a Medal of Honour. By means of tireless tree-to-tree fighting, our men had advanced far enough to be reasonably sure of the location of the well and the troops that guarded it. To push on in the face of such odds meant heavy casualties and perhaps failure. The support of the *Marblehead's* guns was essential.

Half way to the well there was a high hill that was not wooded. Quick volunteered to go up this hill and signal to the ship. He stalked up the slope in full view of the enemy, and there at the top he stood, with his broad back to them, while Spanish bullets peppered the ground all around him, and calmly wigwagged to the *Marblehead* the position of the enemy. The shell fire began, the Spaniards ran for cover, and the Marines, when the woods were cleared, romped in and took Cusco Well. This gave Colonel Huntington control of the entire side of the bay and the naval base was established and held for the fleet.

It is this sort of fighting that appeals to the imagination more than the tedious gnawing of trench warfare or the ponderous movements of great armies. The average American has been brought up on stories of Indian warfare, and it is just this sort of fighting that the Marines have learned to do—have been obliged to do on numerous occasions—the whole force engaged in concerted action to a definite end, and yet each man depending on his own resourcefulness to come through. That this sort of experience helped us when we went in against the highly modernized soldiers of the Kaiser in the Bois de Belleau has already been pointed out in the account of that battle.

Meanwhile, in May, 1898, the Marines were with Dewey at Manila. After the battle of Manila Bay, Marines were landed from the fleet at Cavite to hold the fort and naval station. More Marines were sent to Manila at once, and later Marines served with the Navy in some of the southern islands. At the close of the war a brigade of Marines was left in the Philippines to assist in the work of pacification.

Since that time, though the United States has not until now been actually at war with any nation, the Marines have seen plenty of service, not only in the Philippines and in Mexico, but elsewhere.

The name of General L. W. T. Waller, now in command of the Advance Base Brigade at Philadelphia, is one to conjure with among the Marines. It was Waller, then a Major, who, at the outbreak of the Boxer uprising in China, in 1900, was rushed over from the Philippines with two battalions of Marines —between 800 and 1,000 men—to coöperate with the Army in the safeguarding of American lives and interests. Later they were reinforced by Marines sent from the United States. They participated in the battle of Tien Tsin, the march on Peking, and the relief of the besieged American Legation. Here is the story as printed in the *Indianapolis Sun:*

"It was in the campaign of the allies against the Boxers in 1900. They had captured Tien Tsin by a hard three-day battle. A conference had been called of all the commanders to discuss the question of advancing or waiting for reinforcements. General Robert Meade, in command of the United States Marines, was ill, and Major Littleton W. T. Waller was the junior officer of the representatives of many nations in the conference.

"One by one the older men gave their opinions that there was no pressing need of an advance and that the troops must have several more days of recuperating. Finally Major Waller's opinion was asked, and he stood up and said:

" 'Gentlemen, I don't know what the rest of you mean to do, but the Marines start for Peking at 6 o'clock in the morning.'

"The Marines did start at 6 o'clock in the morning, taking the allies along."

It was Waller who, in October, 1901, took a battalion of Marines down to Samar, one of the untamed islands of the Philippines, to clean it up. It was a wild country, where no white troops had ever before been, filled with hostile savages, and much cut up by streams and jungle. They were misled by their native guides, were lost in the wilderness, and suffered untold privations. A number of men died on that march, but Waller brought his battalion through, marching clear across the island.

Meanwhile I was leading a quiet life. I went to the Philippines in 1902, established the post in Honolulu in 1903, and came home in 1904. But the Marines were not idle. There were troubles in Africa, Korea, Santo Domingo, and Panama that required attention. About 1905 things got pretty messy in the West Indies, and some troops from Panama were sent over to Santo Domingo. In May, 1906— I was a Major then—I was sent down with a battalion of Marines to relieve these troops. I remember I was in New York at the time, on duty in the Navy Yard. At 11 o'clock one night I received orders to report in Philadelphia the next afternoon, and that evening we were putting out to sea on the *Dixie*. Things had quieted down a bit and we were not obliged to make any landings. We stuck around until matters had been straightened out, and were about ready to return home when the revolution broke out in Cuba.

Again the Marines were first on the job, and the troops from the *Dixie* were the first to set foot on Cuban soil. In September four battalions of Marines were rushed down to hold things steady until the

Army of Cuban Pacification could be got ready. The first of the Marines were landed at Cienfuegos; later others went to Havana. By the time the Army got there we had established our bases and I had detachments all along the railroads and the situation well in hand.

There were 2,000 Marines in Cuba when the Army came. Then half of them were withdrawn, leaving one regiment of about 1,000 men which served with the Army throughout the occupation until January, 1909. I was among those who remained. I was stationed at Santo Domingo, in Santa Clara province, in the centre of the island, and our job was to disarm insurgents and keep things quiet.

One incident in connection with the first period of the occupation is worth recording as illustrative of the resourcefulness and fighting spirit of the Marines. It was in the last days of September, 1906, after our landing in Cuba. The *Newark*, of the battleship fleet, was sent to the port of Nuevitas and Marines were landed. Captain (now Lieutenant-Colonel) Harlee, with a detachment of Marines, worked his way up to Camaguey, a town in the interior of the island, where a rebel general with 3,000 troops was reported to be operating outside the town.

The frightened mayor of Camaguey sent word that the insurgents were shooting up the town and terrorizing the inhabitants. Captain Harlee took twenty-five men and went in to clean it up. He divided his little force into patrol squads and went through the streets, stopping and disarming parties of rebels wherever he met them, no matter what their numbers might be. The twenty-five Marines took care of several hundred insurgents in this way, and not entirely without resistance.

At one point a villainous-looking negro Captain came riding up on horseback at the head of a band of his ruffians. The Sergeant in command of the squad of Marines stepped up and ordered him to dismount and disarm. By way of reply the Captain drew and cocked his revolver. The Sergeant promptly clubbed his rifle and smashed the stock over the rebel's hard head, and the party threw down their arms. Captain Harlee gathered in a pile of machetes as high as his waist, and sent back the report that the trouble was over.

After the government had been turned back to the Cubans, and just before the American troops were withdrawn, I took a leading part in a memorable ceremony. We were drawn up in the public square of the town for a sort of farewell tableau. The mayor and town council came out with great dignity and made speeches, and then they impressively presented me with a huge diploma, gorgeous with gilt, in which I was informed that I had been voted *hijo adoptivo* —an adopted son—of Santo Domingo, Cuba. That diploma is to-day one of my valued possessions.

Marines were used during the next few years in Panama, Nicaragua, China, and elsewhere. In March, 1911, at the beginning of the Mexican crisis, a brigade of Marines under Colonel Waller was sent to Guantanamo at the same time the Army was sent to the Border. I commanded a battalion in one of the two regiments sent down. Another regiment was landed from the fleet, making about 2,100 men in all.

During those anxious days people at home were criticizing the Government for taking a foolish risk and were worrying over the apparent lack of protection. I wonder how many of them knew that as large a force of fighting Marines as had ever been gathered together in one body was right there on the job, ready to jump into Vera Cruz at a moment's notice. And I wonder how many Americans realized how capable those Marines were of coping with a situation which seemed fraught with such peril to our arms. A landing at Vera Cruz was not deemed necessary at that time, however, and so but little was heard of the Marines. The chief interest was with the boys who were sent down to the Border. We spent four months at target practice, sham battles, and general training, and then we came home.

In September, 1911, I started on a three-years' cruise with the North Atlantic Fleet, visiting European waters in 1912. During that time I missed some rather interesting affairs in Nicaragua, Haiti, and elsewhere, of which I think I should speak more at length, but before my cruise period was ended I was fortunate enough to have some part in the occupation of Vera Cruz in 1914.

CHAPTER XV

VERA CRUZ AND THE OUTBREAK OF WAR

OF THE activities of the Marines during my absence on cruise, a few seem worth telling here. They had some exciting times in Cuba during the coloured revolution of 1912-13. In February, 1913, the fleet went down to look things over and a brigade of Marines was landed at Guantanamo under Colonel Karmany. They engaged in some lively skirmishes with the rebels among the iron mines and plantations at Santiago de Cuba and returned in May.

It must be remembered that such events took place while the United States was at peace and her people were largely interested in economic questions and domestic politics. I sometimes wonder how many Americans realize that hardly a year has passed during which the Marines have not been fighting somewhere under trying circumstances, perhaps dying under the tropic sun, to uphold the honour of the Flag. The Marines, at least, have never for long suffered from the debilitating effects of peace, and when the Great War came their sword was sharpened and unsheathed.

Did you know, for example, that four good American lives were lost and several United States Marines were wounded in Nicaragua in 1912? The revolutionary situation in that country had become acute and American life and property were unsafe. So they sent the Marines. They fought and they pacified the country. Major Butler took a battalion over to Corinto, Nicaragua, from Panama, and Colonel Pendleton was sent down with a regiment from the States to join him. For the rather stirring events of that campaign, I am indebted to the following account which appeared in the *New York Sun:*

"Early in August of 1912 a battalion of Marines, consisting of ten officers and 338 men, under Colonel Joseph H. Pendleton, U.S.M.C., was ordered from Panama to Nicaragua, then in the throes of a revolution that menaced the lives of American citizens and other peaceful foreigners in that country. That expeditionary force of Marines had to struggle against all the handicaps of a tropical climate, dense forests, and a foe that offered a good deal of stubborn resistance.

"They participated in the bombardment of Managua, a night ambuscade in Masaya, the surrender of General Mena and his rebel army at Granada, the surrender of the rebel gunboats *Victoria* and *Ninety-three*, the assault and capture of Coyotepe, the defence of Paso Caballos Bridge, besides doing garrison and other duty at Corinto, Chinandega, and elsewhere. The most noteworthy event of the campaign was the assault and capture of Coyotepe, which resulted in the crushing of the revolution and the restoration of peace to Nicaragua.

"The assault lasted for more than half an hour under heavy fire from the rebels, who enjoyed a position deemed well-nigh impregnable. During these operations three enlisted men were killed and several wounded. . . .

"The victory at Coyotepe Hill was the climax of other work in which the Marines showed their adaptability and the manner in which they have taken to heart the lessons learned in time of peace. They took the locomotives and the battered rolling stock which the revolutionists had tumbled into the ditches and got them back upon the rails, which the Marines also repaired.

"With this done it was but a short task for these shifty men to get up steam in the funny-looking engines. Then, with the cars loaded with field guns and ammunition and the men anxious for action, the trains staggered along the sinuous track and over an uncertain roadbed, carrying to the front a certainty of defeat for the entrenched foe, safe, as he thought, behind unassailable defences."

Meanwhile, matters had been going from bad to worse in Mexico, and from 1913 on the Marines were closely watching developments in that perturbed country. In January, 1914, the Advance Base Brigade, consisting of the First and Second Advance Base Regiments of Marines, under the command of the present Major General Commandant, George Barnett, was stationed at Culebra, Porto Rico, for instruction in advance base work as a preparation for whatever serious situation might arise. Again the Marines were ready. This brigade returned to the United States just in time to be diverted from the home stations to Vera Cruz, where perhaps the most important action since the Spanish War took place.

It so happened, however, that there were other Marines in Vera Cruz ahead of the Advance Base Brigade. These were the Marines who were aboard the ships of the Atlantic Fleet. The *Utah* and *Florida* were lying in the harbour at Vera Cruz and the *Minnesota* at Tampico; the remainder of the Atlantic Fleet was at target practice off the Chesapeake Capes. I was on the *Arkansas* at the time, and we received orders to hasten at once to Vera Cruz. We sailed on April 17th and arrived in the harbour early in the morning of April 22nd.

Meanwhile, on April 21st, Admiral Fletcher decided to land and take charge of the custom house at Vera Cruz, in order to prevent the German ship *Yperanga*, which lay in the harbour, from landing her cargo of arms and ammunition. The Marines from the *Florida* and *Utah* and the sailor battalions from the two ships were landed under command of Captain W. R. Rush, U. S. N. Lieutenant Colonel W. C. Neville was in command of the Marines. There were about 200 Marines in the landing party and some 300 or 400 sailors.

It was a ticklish business, for there were at least 600 Mexican troops in the town, in addition to the garrison and other attachés of the Naval Academy there. The Mexicans had also set free and armed all the convicts in the vicinity, and there was no way of estimating the number of armed and desperate ruffians abroad.

The custom house was taken over quietly and without great difficulty by this landing force. Soon, however, the Mexican troops and civilians opened fire, and it became necessary to send reinforcements.

The fleet arrived in the harbour at 2 A. M. on April

22nd, and the Marines and sailor battalions were immediately landed. I was in command of the Marines, numbering about 1,000 men, and Captain E. A. Anderson, U. S. N., was in command of the sailors.

The fire of the Mexicans became more intense, and on the morning of the 22nd we were ordered to take Vera Cruz and drive the Mexicans out. At 7:30 we commenced to clean up the town.

The battalion of Marines under Major Butler, which had been sent up from Panama some time before, was landed under fire early in the morning and took part in the occupation of the city. The second Advance Base Regiment, under Lieutenant Colonel C. G. Long, arrived and was landed during the forenoon, so that we had some 2,000 Marines ashore, besides the sailors. About ten American ships lay in the harbour.

I don't know how fully that engagement has been reported to American readers. It was a hot fight while it lasted. The enemy was well supplied with machine guns and the housetops were alive with snipers. It looked like a dive into a hail-storm of bullets, but we took a reef in our belts and started in.

The sailors got it worse than we did, for they started on a rush through the streets, swept by the enemy's fire, and their casualties were numerous. The Marines, with their training in Indian warfare, took another course. Since the open streets were dangerous, we promptly decided to go through the houses, and our chief weapon was the pick-ax.

The streets of Vera Cruz are lined with rows of adjoining houses of adobe with flat roofs and with their fronts picturesquely stained in various colours. The walls of some of them were two or three feet thick, but that did not deter us. We would place a machine gun at the end of a street to keep it clear of Mexicans, and then start in at the first house and go right up the line, breaking through the walls of one house after another, and cleaning each one up as we got to it.

There were Mexicans on the flat housetops that extended the length of the street, but we sent men up to engage them from behind the parapets. This double form of attack, from in front and below, was not to their liking, and we soon had them running for safer cover. When we got to a cross street we rushed across to the house on the opposite side and began again, potting Greasers as we went. It proved to be an effective method, for we cleared out our share of the town that day and in the morning's fighting we had only one man killed.

By 8 o'clock that night we had control of the town, and on April 23rd the whole of Vera Cruz was in the hands of the Americans, though there was considerable sniping from the housetops for several nights. Five lives were lost in the fighting of those two days and a number of men were wounded.

Colonel J. A. Lejeune arrived and took command of all Marines on shore. The town was divided into districts, with the sailors in charge of part of the town and my regiment the remainder. The two

Advance Base Regiments took charge of the outposts, one battalion going to Tejar, where the water
supply of the city was located. This was about
eight miles from the city on the narrow gauge railroad.

Ten days later the Army arrived, and with them
another regiment of Marines under command of
Colonel F. J. Moses. The sailors and fleet Marines
then returned on board their ships, most of which
remained in the harbour all summer. Colonel Waller
arrived about this time and took command of the
Marine brigade, and Colonels Lejeune and Mahoney
took command of the two Advance Base Regiments.
Marines took part in all the subsequent military
activities incident to the American occupation, the
three regiments under Colonel Waller remaining on
duty with about 5,000 Army troops until Vera Cruz
was evacuated in November. I came north in
September, having won my Medal of Honour.

During this period other Marines were watchfully
waiting on the west coast. Colonel Pendleton
assembled the Fourth Regiment at the Marine base
at Mare Island, Cal., and embarked on the *South
Dakota*, *West Virginia*, and *Jupiter* for duty off
the Mexican coast, but conditions did not require
a landing.

In operations of this sort, the Marines are generally
given two chief duties to perform. Because of their
mobility and training, they are usually the first
to make a landing and pave the way for the soldiers
or sailors, and this skirmish work requires speed,

energy, and resourcefulness. It is difficult, perhaps, for the civilian to picture such a situation as has often existed in the experience of the Marines. The ships steam into the harbour with orders to straighten out the difficulties existing on shore, to protect American lives and property, and to take such action as the commanding officer judges to be necessary. But accurate information as to conditions on shore is not always available. The strength and disposition of the enemy or the trouble makers is not definitely known. So Marines are landed to make the necessary reconnaissance. They proceed unfalteringly in the face of the unknown, confident of their ability to do what Marines have done before. Often this reconnaissance is sufficient to quell the disorders, and the report goes back to Washington, "The Marines have landed and have the situation well in hand." Those few words may cover a tale of bloodshed as thrilling as a page of Dumas, but all the American newspaper reader knows is that Uncle Sam's policemen have again somehow managed to break up one of those opera bouffe disorders somewhere south of Key West, and he goes to bed with his sense of security undisturbed.

Thus the Marines are landed, and when the situation is well in hand they proceed to the second of their duties, which is that of provost and patrol work. Naval and Army officers have learned by experience that no one can do that like the Marines, and the Marines are nearly always assigned to the important if not always glorious task of keeping order. That is what they did in Vera Cruz during the summer of 1914. And it is not merely the fractious native that needs restraint; Jack ashore is often a troublesome handful. The sailor will fight the soldier who interferes with his liberties, but he will usually submit to arrest at the hands of a Marine without resistance, for the Marine is his brother-in-arms. The sailor calls the Marine a leatherneck, but he loves him just the same.

When the war broke out in Europe in August, 1914, the United States Marines were not among those who were slumbering in perilous unpreparedness. They were busy on both coasts of Mexico, two regiments were in Santo Domingo and Haiti, and the whole Corps was mobilized and growing. During that same year, 1914, Colonel Charles A. Doyen had the Fifth Regiment of Marines under arms on board the transport *Hancock*, which remained in Santo Domingan waters until December, during a period of unrest in that unfortunate island. Again, in April, 1916, Marines were sent down to Santo Domingo and cleaned out the rebels with the loss of several officers and men. Colonel Pendleton was placed in command of a brigade of Marines which established a sort of military protectorate over the government of the island.

A similar expedition was sent to Haiti in the summer of 1915 under General Waller. He landed with a brigade of Marines in the midst of one of the most serious revolutions in the history of the island. He discovered that the northern part of the island was in the hands of bandit chieftains who used the people for their own ends, and the Government was powerless to restore order. It appeared necessary to wipe out these robber barons, and Waller did it. There was some hard fighting, and I cannot say how many rebels were executed as a military necessity, but Haiti, the whole island, was cleaned up and quieted down and peace was at last restored. Major (now Colonel) Butler was left in Haiti with a number of Marine officers and men to keep the peace. They are still there at this writing, having formed the Haitian constabulary of natives under officers of the United States Marines.

Both Santo Domingo and Haiti were clean jobs, well done. Doubtless some of the Marines down there would give a year's pay to be with the boys in France, but a Marine learns that duty is duty, whether he is picked to serve as a runner under fire on the Marne or is fated to serve as an office orderly at Marine Headquarters in Washington. It's all in his day's work.

As to my own part in this troubled period prior to the entrance of the United States in the Great War, I was doing what I could to get ready. The Corps was expanding and there was a great need for officers. I came north in September, 1914, from Vera Cruz, and my three-year cruise period was over in October. I was relieved of my sea command by Colonel Fuller and went to Portsmouth, N. H., in December, to take command of the prison there. Seeing the clouds of war approaching, and feeling the need to

fit myself for wider service, I went to Fort Leavenworth to study in September, 1916, and later to the
War College at Washington. I graduated from
the War College in the spring of 1917, at about the
time the United States entered the war, and received
my Colonel's commission.

The Corps was at this time organized in the customary manner and engaged in its customary activities. The Marines are always on a war-time footing;
there is nothing that may properly be called a peace
basis with us. But the United States is not often
at war, and under ordinary conditions our forces
are distributed up and down our coasts and over the
Seven Seas. There are always some of our men on
board ship, while the rest are posted at the various
Naval Stations. The dreadnaughts commonly carry
about eighty-five Marines and the smaller battle-
ships about seventy-five, with usually two officers
to each detachment. The larger cruisers carry a
sergeant's guard.

The centre of activity of the Marines at home is
in Philadelphia, where is located the headquarters
of what we call our Advance Base Brigade. It is
here that the hurry calls come when the Marines are
needed. The General Headquarters is in Washington. At Paris Island, near Port Royal, S. C., and
at Mare Island, Cal., are situated our training stations where the recruits receive fourteen weeks of
training. At Miami, Fla., we have the Marine
aviation grounds.

Not to go too far back into history, the Marine

Corps at the outbreak of the Spanish War numbered 1,800. It was increased temporarily to 4,500 at that time, and afterward, in March, 1899, to 5,000. On different subsequent occasions, to meet the demands of an expanding Navy, the numbers were increased to 7,500, 9,500, and more, until at the outbreak of the Great War we had 14,500.

Owing to the kind of work we have had to do and the size of the detachments commonly engaged, we have always maintained a good complement of trained officers. Though we are soldiers and not sailors, our association has always been with the Navy and Naval men have sought our ranks. In 1883 for the first time an Annapolis man became an officer of Marines. From about that time until 1898 all our new officers were graduates of the Naval Academy. Then the Navy was expanded and needed them all, and the Marines were forced to look elsewhere for their officers. Since then a few Naval Academy graduates have received commissions in the Marine Corps, but the majority of our officers now are not Annapolis men, and we have developed our own system of officer training.

Up to 1916 the highest officers of Marines, with the exception of the Major General Commandant, were the Colonels. In August, 1916, we were allowed by Congress four general officers in addition to the Major General, and Waller, Lejeune, Pendleton, and Cole were commissioned Brigadier Generals. Since the Marines have taken part in the fighting in France, others have received this rank. Major General

George Barnett, our present Commandant, received his four-year appointment in 1913 and was reappointed in 1917.

When at last the United States declared war against Germany, the Marine Corps was in fine fettle, but in one respect we were, like the rest of the country, unprepared for the great task that lay ahead of us. We lacked man power, but we immediately set about repairing that lack. President Wilson was empowered to increase the Corps to 17,500 if necessary, and this he promptly did. Then Congress voted an expansion to 30,000 for the period of the war, and again in July, 1918, raised the figure to 75,000. Recruiting was stimulated and the numbers climbed steadily up to nearly 60,000, when enlistments were halted on October 1, 1918, pending the consideration of the Man Power Bill, and for a time the ranks were filled by induction from the draft. On December 5th recruiting was resumed for voluntary enlistments for the four-year period.

Following the first action of Congress, the Marines started a whirlwind recruiting campaign. We did not lower our requirements one jot, for we knew that no weakling could be made into a Marine. The whole Corps was on its toes, for there was promise of action, and the Marine lives on action. The United States was going across to get into the biggest thing that had ever happened, and the Marine recognizes no place but the van. Marine Headquarters in Washington was a beehive, our publicity men were on their job, and the recruiting Sergeants were talking their devoted heads off. As a result, the young men of America flocked to our standard and in those days we drew in some of the best blood in the land. Some of our old-timers were made non-commissioned officers and we sent in a bid for the first of the Plattsburg graduates. The Corps underwent a period of rapid expansion, but we were able to absorb the new elements as fast as they came along.

The new recruits were sent first to our regular training camps at Paris Island and Mare Island. There they were jammed through the regulation fourteen-weeks period of preliminary training, which in some instances was shortened for the emergency. When they came out of that school of unremitting drill they were Marines.

At the outbreak of war the Corps leased land at Quantico, Va., on the Potomac River some thirty-five miles south of Washington, and set about establishing a finishing-off and embarkation camp. Major Campbell was sent down from Annapolis to take charge. As soon as the recruits had been whipped into shape at Paris and Mare Islands they were sent in detachments to Quantico, where they were organized into companies.

Up to this time the Marines had had no fixed regimental organization, provisional regiments or battalions having been formed temporarily when the emergency arose. Now we were confronted with the problem of forming a complete military organization on the plan of the United States Army for the period of the war. Aside from the officers, we had, as a nucleus in each regiment, fifty or sixty non-commissioned officers who were experienced Marines. All the privates in the regiments formed at Quantico were new men.

By the time the Marine Corps had climbed up to 30,000 strong, some 5,000 more than were in the Regular Army at the outbreak of the Spanish War, several regiments had been formed. The First, Second, Third, and Fourth were on duty in the West Indies, and about this time some small ones were sent down there. The Seventh, under Colonel Shaw, went to Guantanamo; the Eighth, under Colonel Moses, went to Galveston; the Ninth was sent to Cuba, Colonel James Mahoney being in command of the brigade of three regiments. The Fifth and Sixth were organized at Quantico and were the ones destined for service in France.

About June 1, 1917, I was made Commandant of the Post at Quantico and went down to take charge. The First Battalion of the Fifth Regiment had already been formed when I arrived, and new detachments were coming right along to fill up the regiment. They were all living in tents then, and while the training was going forward we were erecting cantonments, a target range, and all the other appurtenances of a permanent post. Major Evans was my right-hand man in charge of organization, and he was a wonder. Major Ellis was sent down as my assistant in charge of instruction. Later the officers' school was sent up from Norfolk, and we had charge of that also. Of the life at Quantico I shall speak more at length in the next chapter.

I remained in charge of the post there until September, when I was relieved by General Lejeune and embarked for France at the head of the Sixth Regiment. And the curtain was rung up on the stirring drama I have endeavoured to describe.

CHAPTER XVI

The Making of a Marine

WHEN the Great War swept the United States into its vortex, the Marine Corps was already on a war footing and they got their new units quickly into shape. The Marines were disciplined, dependable troops the day they landed in France. That is why they were called upon to perform all that tedious provost duty and keep the other troops in order. And by the time they had completed their French training in camp and in the trenches they were seasoned soldiers. This was not the result of mere chance, though we were unquestionably fortunate in the matter of personnel. It was the result of a thorough and intensive system of training and instruction which we believe is as good as any in the world, and I should like to tell something of the way we make Marines out of the raw material. We took boys fresh from college and business offices and put them through the mill, and in less than a year they were fighting in France with all the dash and snap and spirit of old members of the Corps. Young men who had never shot a rifle or killed anything more dangerous than a chicken were turned into such fighters that the whole world heard of them. Perhaps a glimpse at the system of training will give some idea of how it was accomplished.

Young men are attracted to the Marine Corps from all walks of life. In ordinary times the service has been for three years and has proved attractive to the best type of American youth. The Marine service has always been popular and the percentage of reënlistment has been high. A larger organization than formerly is now being planned and the selective enlistment of men for a four-year period is now going on. It is still possible to become a Marine—if you're man enough.

Our standards have always been high in the matter of physique, intelligence, and character. We have sought for men above the average in physical strength and agility. We have sought intelligent, educated men, for we have learned that they have sense enough to realize the necessity for obedience. They get the idea of the discipline quicker than the other sort and it stands by them in a pinch.

The recruits which we took in for the overseas service were of an even higher quality than the average in previous years. The campaign was, of course, stimulated by the war, and we soon had bunches of fine fellows on their way to the training stations at Paris Island, S. C., and Mare Island, Cal.

At these stations the recruit undergoes fourteen weeks of intensive training. For the war emergency this period was shortened to six or eight weeks in many instances, after which the men were sent on to Quantico to be polished off. We knew there would be still more rigid training in France before they would be considered fit to fight.

The recruit takes his preliminary oath and is sent to quarantine, where he is subjected to general inspection and physical examination. At the close of the quarantine period he is re-examined and takes the full oath of allegiance. He then goes "over the fence" into the training camp. There used to be a fence at Paris Island, but the phrase is only traditional now.

Here the men are grouped eight men to a squad and eight squads to a company and are put through the regulation military drill. They become acquainted with the field work on the manœuvre grounds, they learn how to take care of their equipment and adjust their packs "Marine style," they become accustomed to all the rules and regulations of cantonment life. They learn the meaning of neatness and the importance of "police work." Finally, when they have been whipped into some sort of shape, the drill in markmanship is begun at the rifle ranges, and this drill is kept up until the recruit is worthy to take his place in the ranks of the sharpest shooting organization in the world.

The Marine Corps's reputation for marksmanship can hardly be overemphasized, and it is all due to the training. Over 67 per cent. of the entire Corps have qualified as marksmen, sharpshooters, or expert riflemen, the three grades established for proficiency. Toward the close of a recent report on the work of the Marines, Secretary Daniels said:

"Thus it is that the United States Marines have fulfilled the glorious traditions of their Corps in this their latest duty as the 'soldiers who go to sea.' Their sharpshooting—and in one regiment 93 per cent. of the men wear the medal of a marksman, a sharpshooter, or an expert rifleman—has amazed soldiers of European armies, accustomed merely to shooting in the general direction of the enemy. Under the fiercest fire they have calmly adjusted their sights, aimed for their man, and killed him, and in bayonet attacks their advance on machine-gun nests has been irresistible."

Much of the recruit's progress is due to the labours of the drill Sergeant, who is usually a man who bears about with him a perpetual grouch because he is not at the front killing Germans. The mental attitude thus produced is well calculated to carry the fear of authority into the heart of the unbroken American. It is good for his soul.

A list of all the daily duties of the young recruit would make tedious reading, but it seems to have impressed a correspondent of the Savannah *News*, who wrote as follows in an article describing the life at Paris Island:

"What a man who has passed through the Marine training can't do isn't worth mentioning. He is trained to box, to wrestle, and has bayonet practice, and when it comes to washing dishes and peeling potatoes—well, as one Marine wrote to a certain Savannah friend, 'When I get through my training here I would make any man a good wife.'"

And during these weeks, from the first minute, the recruit is shot full of the spirit of the Corps, and gradually there dawns upon his intellect the fact that there exists among the Marines a code of thought and faith and conduct which, like the British constitution, is all-potent though unwritten.

After this preliminary training has been completed, with its hikes and company drills, its shooting and its bayonet practice, the young Marine is sent on to Quantico, where there are facilities for the advanced training of over 10,000 men. Here there are manœuvre grounds and rifle ranges of the most modern type. The men attend school where the best instructors obtainable teach topography, machine gun work, military science, and all the rest of it, and tactical marches are required to teach the men the best use of the roads.

In one section of the camp there are hills and ridges and valleys that closely resemble the battleground of Vimy Ridge, and here the practice trenches are located. They are dug 450 yards apart and are fitted with wire entanglements and all the features of actual warfare. The Germans are represented by dummies and against them the young Marines direct their machine gun fire. Mines are sprung, wires are cut, and over-the-top charges are indulged in, with a bloodless mopping up at the end. The rifle, the automatic, the bayonet, and the grenade are all used in the manner required by actual fighting, and woe to the man who lags behind or shoots wild.

Never having been through the private's training

myself, I must rely upon some one else to present the recruit's view of it, which is naturally more interesting than that of his officers. The following letters were written by a Marine, now a Sergeant, who passed through the training at Paris Island and Quantico in 1918. Reading between the lines, one catches a vision of the unfolding of the Marine spirit.

Paris Island, S. C.,
July —, 1918.

Dear Dad:—

Here I am in the Y. M. C. A. at Quarantine Station, Marine Barracks, Paris Island. I am writing to-night because to-morrow and the next day we get our physical examinations, which will take up all of our time. Then we "cross the line" as they call it and all of the men I came down here with will be formed into a company.

We had a long, dusty trip in a day coach, and the best dressed man in the crowd (that's me) was surely a sight. I made a bundle out of my coat, collar, and tie and put them in my suitcase. I was covered with cinders and grime and my long hair was tousled. My long hair is no more, dad. You should see my Mr. Zip haircut.

Well, we landed in Port Royal, a town inhabited chiefly by Civil War history. A Sergeant took us in charge and we walked the gangplank of a small steamer tug named *Pilot Boy*. I saw the ocean for the first time, dad, and real live dolphins. We arrived at Paris Island in about twenty minutes, but not before we had had a lot of fun bidding good-bye to the mainland. Most of us threw our hats into the channel where the tide, rapidly receding, carried them out to sea. On the dock a Marine Sergeant took us in charge and we started the mile hike to Quarantine Station, a huge camp where all the applicants must come for examination, preliminary instruction, and formation into companies. This Sergeant was a regular bull for strength. He seemed a powerful man and his voice was just as powerful. They call them "leather-lungs" down here. He was not unkind, though, and seemed to gaze upon us with a sort of half-hearted pity for what might be in store for us. In fact, he told us we were not going to a picnic and that we had better "snap out of it" right from the start, all of which he assured us would make things easier.

I learned what "snap out of it" means, to-day, when I didn't hear my name at roll call, and two Corporals came out looking for me. They found me, dad; they found me! One of them looked at me with a degree of disgust in his eyes, the like of which I had never seen, and said, "So you expect to be a Marine? Well, you can't be a Marine and be a dope. Snap out of it!" I am here to tell you I snapped. In fact, I have been snapping all day. It seems to be the principal occupation here.

But last night was a sort of reception night. As we came into camp we were met by hundreds of fellows in white pajamas who had arrived the day before. They all wanted to know the home state of each one of us and we were all busy shouting our cities and names. Many of the boys found old friends or made new ones. We were given new white pajamas, furnished with soap and towels, directed to a shower bath, and then lined up for chow. That is food, dad, and wonderful food it was. Was I hungry? And did I eat? I never knew I could eat a meal like that. You know I have always been a light eater.

After we had tried to eat everything in sight and had

failed, we went out and saw the camp. There are lots of queer trees and palmettoes here. There are cotton fields with old negro mammies hoeing and a line of red-sailed fishing boats come and go with the tide in the channel, putting out to sea. Last night we saw three destroyers painted a dull grey steaming out to sea in a heavy smoke screen.

As soon as it was dark we went to the movies which the Y. M. C. A. conducts in the open air. We sat on the soft sand which was still warm from the sun and a delightful sea breeze swept continuously over this motley audience hailing from all parts of the United States and representing every class and type. Strange bits of slang and colloquial phrases came to me from every side. It was an evening potent with promise of great interest in this new, strange life of the Marines. Under the starry canopy, from the great shadows of this island night, came the roar of the tide, sharp sounds of distant commands, far-off strains from tented quartets, and the faint tinkle of pots and pans from the galleys where men were preparing for the next morning's breakfast. I went to bed in my newly assigned bunk and scarcely slept a wink for thinking and wondering what my part would be in the great business of becoming a Marine.

This morning after chow we went into an open-air pavilion and heard Captain Denby give his famous talk on what was expected of us as Marines. Captain Denby is an ex-Congressman from Michigan, and he surely must have been an easy victor in his race for office, for he held us all spellbound as he described the duties of a Marine— where a Soldier of the Sea must go, what he is expected to do, how he must conduct himself, and the penalty imposed in war time for touching a drop of intoxicating liquor. Truth and the *esprit de corps* of the Marines seemed to be the theme of this oracle whom they call the "Daddy" of the Marine Corps. They all went up to him after it was over—all those who could get near him—just to shake hands and hear a few words more. A lot of the fellows who had lied when they enlisted went up to square themselves, and the Captain looked more like he might be their own father than either a Congressman or a Captain of Marines. He is a big man in stature as well as spirit. Even I, who have learned to respect the uniform of Marine officers with a respect born of confidence and esteem, forgot that Denby was anything so formidable as a Captain, and I told him all about you and your fight for the City Council last fall. He put his arm around my shoulder and his face lit up with all the enthusiasm of a man who knows men and loves them from the bottom of his heart. This, I think, will prove to be one of the biggest experiences of my camp life, for then and there I resolved to be a Marine in every sense of the word, first, last, and all the time, and try to uphold the splendid traditions of the Corps.

Love to all,

BILL.

The word "snap" to which Bill refers is one of the most widely used and significant at Paris Island. It is descriptive of the spirit and technique which the drill Sergeants endeavour to instill into the minds of the new recruits who are learning foot drill without rifles. This is the way one recruit described it:

So precise and snappy is the drill of the Marines that the new man, who has always considered himself quite alert, finds it necessary to make himself all over again.

His chief slogan becomes "snap." The word is synonymous with "pep," but it means infinitely more, for every movement in the Marine Corps must be executed quickly and at exactly the right time, and, after the training has become a science, at the same time.

Even the eyes seem to snap when a Marine commander gives the command, "Eyes right!" As a result, Marine drill is an almost perfect mechanism, moving in well-ordered clicks, quickly, to the accomplishment of its purpose.

Even in hours of play in the company streets the men, with that rare humour of imitation, often regulate their actions by shouting commands, or if at work, count a cadence—"*One*, two, three, four; *one*, two, three, four!" —as they fold their clothes or rake the ground about their tents. In this spirit of fun they snap from one position to another.

One Marine who, just before taps, drilled up and down the street in his pajamas giving bogus commands and obeying them himself, was caught later talking in his sleep, giving the same commands in a voice calculated to imitate his superior officer. Naturally he became the laughing-stock of his "buddies," who considered his sleep-walking better than the one in Macbeth.

At the movies these hardy "buck" privates will count "*One*, two, three, four; *one*, two, three, four!" as the hero marches toward the leading lady, and if he does not embrace her with true Marine speed, they will shout, "Snap out of it!"

Yes, snap is the word from the time the boys "hit the deck" or get up in the morning, through their drill periods, not forgetting chow, until they make down their immaculate bunks at the sound of taps. Snap is the first thing the Marine learns and the last he forgets. It is the Marine snap that has won for the Corps the well-deserved reputation of being the snappiest fighting force in the world.

Here is Bill's second letter to his father:

Paris Island, S. C.,
July —, 1918.

DEAR DAD:—

Three nights ago we came almost the entire length of Paris Island, six miles, to the Manœuvre Grounds, or Boot Camp as it is called. We have no rifles yet and won't have for ten days or more. You see the camps are arranged in a loop. When you have gone around the loop at Paris Island you are a Marine. That's what the Sergeant said yesterday and I'm beginning to believe him. If I have any muscles in my body which haven't been stretched within the last week it isn't the fault of the drill Sergeant or the physical instructor.

I've been swimming twice. There's nothing like the ocean, Dad. You know I used to do my two miles a day in the lake. Well, a five-mile swim would be easy here only they won't let you try to swim that far. Our company went down in a column of squads uniformed in regulation Marine Corps bathing suits.

Already we drill fairly well, but there are still a few who don't seem able to get in step. They are put in an awkward squad and given extra attention by the Sergeant. I'm glad I'm not in that squad.

At the beach we were separated into two classes, those who could swim and those who could not. There is an instructor for every man who cannot swim and chief instructors who supervise the work. Flocks and flocks of pelicans and sea gulls flew over us, evidently much disturbed because we had interfered with their summer homes at the seaside.

I don't think I'll ever work in an office again. I am tanning up fine now and have gained six pounds, so you see exercise agrees with me. My bunkie, who lives in the same tent with me, is a graduate of Oberlin College and was a crack athlete there. We had a field meet yesterday and he won the high jump, broad jump, and quarter mile run. He tells me that though he used to train in college, he never was in such good physical condition as he is down here. It must be the outdoor life and the happy-go-lucky spirit which all the boys have acquired. No matter what hardships spring up or what strenuous duties we have to face, they are all taken up with a laugh. Good cheer always saves the day.

I won't need the toilet kit that Edith is making. The Marine Corps has furnished me with one that will take up much less room, I think. Just take it when she gives it to you and keep it, and I will write and thank her for it. If you were here you would understand that we have no room for excess baggage.

You should see me washing my own clothes. We go over as a company to a place where there are rows of smooth, hard benches which drain into a trough. Each man takes a bucket full of clothes, some washing soap, and a big bristle brush. There are indoor places for washing, but those are used only in bad weather or in winter. It was hard work the first day, but I'm getting used to it now. We scrub clothes about three times a week. After each scrubbing a Corporal in charge inspects every piece of clothing. I never saw a cleaner bunch of men in any one aggregation before. There is something to be cleaned all the time, but there is a great satisfaction in knowing that you are "always ready" (a Marine Corps slogan) and look just like you were on parade. We dress up for our Sergeant the same as we would for a General.

I must go now, for we are going to be instructed in our general orders which will enable us to go on guard duty. We must memorize fifteen or more orders and be able to say them without a moment's hesitation. A Marine must always know these, for he may be called to most any country in the world where the United States has a legation or consulate, to guard our interest there.

There's the Sergeant's whistle, which says, "Fall out and fall in."

Love to all,

BILL.

Other letters from this young Marine, showing the progress of the training, follow:

Paris Island, S. C.,
July—, 1918.

DEAR DAD:—

The day after your visit I was made an "acting Jack" or acting Corporal, which means that at the end of my training here at Paris Island I will be made a regular Corporal. I wear a leather belt now and help to drill my company. I may or may not have to go to the non-commissioned officers' school. I would rather not, for it might mean that I would have to stay on the Island and drill troops, and you know I would rather go across.

The camp has changed a great deal since you were here. It is marvellous the changes a week can bring. New buildings have sprung up everywhere and the entire island is a veritable city.

We are on the range now. I am on the first shift, which has reveille at 4 o'clock while it is still very dark. We have early morning coffee and then hike two miles to the range, drilling every step of the way except for one stretch of road where they give us the "route step." Then we sing and shout to one another. It is a weird sight to see the long columns of companies dressed in old, ragged coats padded heavily at the elbows and shoulders (many of the range coats have no backs), swinging along, singing lustily and handling their rifles with the assurance that comes only with long practice.

As daylight peeps over the targets we begin our fire, which lasts until one o'clock in the afternoon. We shoot rain or shine. When it rains we take our ponchos and roll up in them while waiting our turn on the firing line. On pleasant days there is no shade and the place where my back is exposed to the sun is a deep tan now.

We "snap in" before firing actual bullets. By that I mean we go through all the science of firing; we adjust our windage, peep sight, and elevation, each man according to the instruction of his coach. We "snap in" three or four rounds, then shoot a clip of ammunition at the targets. Each man is assigned to a target which he keeps all through the three weeks of his range work. We shoot rapid fire, ten shots to the minute, at 200 yards, rapid fire at 300 and 500 yards, and slow fire at 300, 500, and 600 yards. Even the large target looks terribly small at 600 yards. Half the battle is keeping the sights well blackened by smoking them in burning shoe polish or oil. Then, too, the bolt must be kept in good condition so it won't jam. Marines are taught the science of shooting with the utmost care. We must calculate everything according to mathematical tables—

elevation, the velocity of the wind, and the "zero" of the rifle. The greatest crime is to shoot carelessly without strict adherence to form. The rifle must be held just so, with the left arm well under the piece, the eye just back of the firing pin, and the jaw set tightly to the butt of the rifle, never firing until the breath is under perfect control so that there is not the slightest possibility of a "wabble."

Very few of the men fail to become marksmen and most of them are sharpshooters and experts, all of which shows what expert coaching will do. Our coaches are mighty good fellows, always kind and patient and anxious to have us make a good showing.

We expect to shove off in three or four days. Where we are going no one has the least knowledge but every one has his own idea, and I have been told that I am going everywhere from Siberia to Texas. Of course Marines go all over the world, so there is a possible grain of truth in each rumour.

More in two or three days.

BILL.

Quantico, Va.,
August —, 1918.

DEAR DAD:—

We arrived at Quantico late night before last. We had to stand in line for about thirty minutes while some one went after the officers of the supply department. They were all up at the Post Gym. to hear Madame Schumann-Heink sing.

This is a real camp. I hope you can get down here before I leave. It is to Paris Island what New York is to Hoboken. I had the equivalent of six meals during the day's trip here from Paris Island. Every one along the road treated us royally. There were lots of nice canteen girls and members of the Red Cross who gave us ice cream, sandwiches, and coffee, and all sorts of bird food which we weren't used to but which tasted mighty good.

The best news I have is that instead of being made a Corporal, as I expected, I have been made a Sergeant and will have charge of a detail of men in one of the bunk houses. At Quantico we get "liberty" every week-end and may run up to Washington for the day at a total cost of a little more than $3. My detail is to be sent out for duty to the miners' and sappers' camp about two miles out on a concrete road. I don't know a thing about the work but will write you all about it as soon as we are settled. There are so many supplies to draw and so much equipment to check up that I haven't much time to write now.

Your Marine,
Bill.

Quantico, Va.,
August —, 1918.

Dear Dad:—

What do you think? I am at Château-Thierry! Not the one in France, but a regular imitation Château-Thierry right here in Virginia. A whole section of the Virginia woodland has been taken over and blasted, dug, and mined by the miners and sappers of the Marine Corps until it is almost an exact replica of the country around Château-Thierry and Vimy Ridge. The Scouts and Snipers stay at Vimy Ridge, which is closer to the main camp than we are. Both places are used as schools and for exhibition purposes. Troops of Marines come through here before going to France and help dig the trenches and take part in the sham battles and patrol raids that are everyday occurrences here.

Most of my detail never saw a mine before, but all of the men in camp here are experienced miners and sappers and have worked for years in the mines in Butte and other Western mining centres. They have been retained here as instructors and will teach us the game of laying a sap through No Man's Land and blowing up the enemy trenches. The Russian sap is used to establish listening posts and can be dug without detection by the enemy.

At Château-Thierry there are three lines of main trenches with their supporting trenches, shelters, dugouts, machine gun nests, barbed wire entanglements, and all the trench accessories realistic as in actual warfare. Next week we are going to blow out the Commander's dugout, which is thirty feet underground and affords sleeping quarters for a platoon of men. It looks just like a hotel, for the hewn walls have been plastered with cement by a cement gunner. It seems a shame to blow it all up. But the officers want to see how much powder it will take and how quickly it is feasible to repair the damage; all of which, I suppose, is one of the many lessons of warfare.

To the novice the science of underground warfare seems interminable. It is also about the most important, it seems to me, for although aviation has proved to be of great assistance in observation and even in direct attacks, there is positively no way for the enemy to detect the grim approach of the sappers and miners who may tunnel to their very door and blow up an entire field with comparative ease.

As soon as we are ready for any specific phase of the work, my detail will undoubtedly be shipped to France, for the Allies stand in great need of this work. But just because I am learning to be a miner, dad, does not mean that I am not a Marine. On the contrary, the officers here seem to be more particular than ever about our appearance, keeping us in good physical shape, and inspecting our equipment. We carry our rifles and packs the same as the other men and hope to see some actual fighting, for our work carries us to the very first line trench and beyond.

I must stop now, for I have made arrangements to go in on the truck to the main camp with one of the boys who is going to entertain his sister and three other girls from Washington at the Hostess House.

Love to all.

BILL.

In Bill's first letter to his father there is a reference to Captain Edwin Denby's address to the recruits at Paris Island. I am inclined to believe that this address does more than any other one thing to awaken the young minds of the recruits to a realization of their responsibility as Marines and to open their eyes to the significance of membership in the historic Corps. It is a vital step in the making of a Marine, the value of which can hardly be overestimated.

Captain Denby is the son of the Minister to China in Cleveland's administration. He served for several terms in Congress and then retired from politics to go into business, in which he was equally successful. But the war spirit got him; he wanted to become a Marine. Turning aside all suggestions that influence might secure for him a commission at the outset, he enlisted as a private and took the training. He rose from the ranks to the Captaincy. He is a big, powerful man and a born orator. His personality is ideal for the task he has undertaken; no one could be better fitted than he to flood the minds and hearts of his hearers with the spirit of the Marines.

He talks to the applicants in the open air, in groups of a hundred, and I am told that the occasion is one to be long remembered by them—the sunshine and the breeze in the palmettoes, and the stretch of blue ocean, and the stirring words of the orator ringing across the sands.

He begins by calling attention to the most serious of all a soldier's crimes—desertion—and the kindred sins of absence over leave and sleeping on post. The penalty, he points out, may be death or some other severe penalty with the loss of citizenship, and he explains why. He passes on to the subject of drunkenness and explains why the Marines have found it best to enforce the rule of no drink at all. He explains the system of pay, allotments, and insurance, counselling thrift. Then he takes up the history of the Corps.

The work of the Corps, in normal times, he says, is not laid down by law or regulation, long custom and experience having shown how the Corps can best serve the Government. The first duty is as guards for the ships of the Navy, with service as soldiers, police, orderlies, and sentinels. This includes police work ashore, the manning and serving of the secondary batteries aboard ship, and the organization of landing parties. Captain Denby calls attention to the cordial relations existing between the sailors and the Marines.

Second, the Marines may be called upon to act as garrisons in overseas possessions of the United States, such as the Philippines. Five hundred Marines were sent to act as the garrison of the Island of St. Thomas the day we took it over from Denmark.

Third, they serve as guards for the Navy yards and all property of the Navy. And, fourth, they serve, in a general way, as the guardians of the Monroe Doctrine—the visible evidence of force and protection for foreigners as well as Americans on the Western Hemisphere.

Captain Denby goes on to describe the *esprit de corps* of the Marines. He tells the recruits what they will have to do and offers some plain truths about plain work. He explains the rules of obedience to officers and non-commissioned officers, the value and meaning of the salute, and the rights of privates. He describes the requirements of the drill and rifle practice. He makes a plea for letters to the folks at home and calls for voluntary censorship. He discusses foul language and profanity, diseases and morals. He expounds the value and meaning of the oath and discusses its various parts. Altogether he sums up in a remarkable way the duties and responsibilities and privileges of the Marines.

Set forth by some men, this sort of thing would be listened to with scant attention. It is a long address; to restless young men it might be a great bore. They would take it all with a grain of salt. Not so with Captain Denby's oratory. The boys listen to him with rapt attention and when it is over they crowd about him for a more personal word and approach him as a father confessor. It is wonderfully impressive and effective, like the official charge at some fraternity initiation.

I think I cannot do better, in closing this chapter on the making of a Marine, than by quoting some of the more striking paragraphs in Captain Denby's address. In my humble opinion they are classic and might be read with profit by others than Marine recruits.

You are down here to enlist in the Marine Corps. You know very little about the Corps. You know more than the average man on the outside because you have talked with recruiting Sergeants and perhaps read literature of the Corps, but that is not saying much. The average man on the outside has a very vague idea as to what the Marine Corps is, and what place it holds in the American military establishment—what it does for the Government, in other words. As a rule he only knows that one day he opens his morning paper and finds that there has been trouble at Vladivostok, Siberia, for instance, and the Marines have landed, and then that phrase we hear so often, "The Marines have the situation well in hand." The next day he notices in his paper that there has been trouble in Central America, or South America perhaps, and again "The Marines have landed and have the situation well in hand." And again he opens his paper and finds that there has been trouble in the Malay Straits

Settlements, or Borneo, or Siam, or some other place long forgotten by God or man, and once more "The Marines have landed and have the situation well in hand." So he says, "Who and what the dickens are these Marines? I never hear of them except when there is trouble somewhere, and then they seem to rise up out of the sea, and they are always landing and always getting situations well in hand." And I don't know but what that is a pretty good description of the United States Marines. They are the stormy petrels of the United States Service. A petrel is a little sea bird that flies on the wings of the storm. So does the Marine, and wherever the storm blows you may count upon finding him.

．　　．　　．　　．　　．　　．

Let me point out to you that there are slackers and slackers. We are accustomed to think of the slacker only as one who fails or refuses to put on his country's uniform when the country needs him for its defence. But there are many other forms of slacking. Some of them are even more objectionable than that, and one of the most offensive forms of slacking is that exhibited by the man in uniform who fails or refuses to perform cheerfully and well whatever duty he is given to do, because he cannot get the duty he wants to do.

．　　．　　．　　．　　．　　．

You must become good shots. The Marine Corps has always been celebrated throughout the world for its marksmanship, and if we ever get to open fighting in France, the Marine Corps will give the greatest exhibition of military marksmanship the world has ever seen. You men must do your part. You can become good shots if you will, and if you fail it will be because you lack the will to succeed. It is almost a mathematical certainty that any man who can pass the surgeon, has good eyesight, sound body, and sound nerves, can learn to shoot well. You will shoot 60 shots. Each shot, if you hit the bulls-eye, counts 5. Five times 60 is 300. Therefore, the highest possible score you can make is 300. No man has ever done it, but why shouldn't you? If you do, you will be famous throughout the Marine Corps, but you don't have to get 300 to become a qualified marksman and to be a good shot. If you get only 202 you will win the privilege of wearing upon your uniform the little silver bar of the marksman, and you will receive $2 additional monthly pay. If you get 238 you will wear the cross of the sharpshooter and get $3 additional monthly pay. If you get 253 you will wear the wreath and crossed rifles of the expert and get $5 additional monthly pay, all for one year. Each year every man shoots for record again. Go to it, men, and take your place as good shots in the best shooting force in the world. One other thing. If you know anything about high-powered rifles now, and have shot big game or at targets on the outside, forget it and go to the range with an empty mind and learn to shoot as the coaches instruct you. They know best how military marksmen are made, and that is the way you must learn.

.   .   .   .   .   .

You will at the end of your training, I hope, find that you have learned four things supremely well—obedience, discipline, how to shoot well, and how to use the rifle with the bayonet. If you will have developed your bodies and made them strong, quick, and hard, and learn those four things, you will be Marines. All things else can be easily built upon that foundation, and all things else that you are required to learn are comparatively easy, once you have thoroughly mastered those four. Those are the four great elements of the foot soldier.

. . . . . .

As you have often been told, we are fighting to make the world a decent place to live in. We are fighting for future generations, for the peace of the yet unborn as well as for ourselves. So must we try hard, that while we fight to make the world a decent place to live in, we do not so conduct ourselves that those who are to be born hereafter will not be fit people to live in a clean and decent world. We of America have stood on the sidelines and watched this ghastly war for three years, and now we are in it. We have read with deep grief of the number of splendid young men of England, France, Canada, and Australia who have had their lives ruined, who have been beaten not by the German foe but by disease behind the lines. Scientists cannot estimate the harm that will be done to future generations on account of the flood of diseased blood that will be poured into the veins of those countries because of these illnesses contracted during this war. We only know that one hundred years hence there will be deformed and misshapen babies born. There will be half-witted men and women. The sum total of human misery will be greatly increased and national efficiency greatly lowered because of the diseases suffered by the boys in the Great War. And we of America have seen it all, and now we are in it too. Shall we not determine that we of the Marine Corps at least shall win both wars? So shall we be glad ever to look back with clean and lofty pride upon our part in this great struggle.

. . . . . .

Then, too, remember this. There is no man of us but has left at home some woman. It may be a mother, a wife, a sister, a daughter, or only a girl. But there is some woman vitally interested in each one of us. Let me say to you that ours is the easy part, no matter what suffering or hardships we have to undergo. You come here to the island and you go through work that is hard and trying, but that only needs a man's spirit in a man's body. And all the while you are learning new things. You are learning the art of the soldier. Your bodies are being built up and there are things of interest constantly coming to your attention. And so it will be throughout all your service, until perhaps you find yourselves on the battlefields of Europe. Even there, amid the horrors of which we have read so much, you will find the curious joy and exaltation of battle. After the guns begin to roll and the first tremor of nervousness is over, you will find the lust of battle to possess you. You will want to get at the enemy. Every man who has ever been under fire knows what I mean. And if the white road of duty shall lead to the soldier's grave, after all, is that so terrible? You will never again have a chance to offer your lives in so noble a cause. All through your service you will have the pride and glory of the thought that you are offering all for humanity and for your country, and that is enough to make things seem easy. You may think me childish. Perhaps I am, but to me the sight of the flag takes the hurt and the pain out of most things. To me the flag seems like some beautiful spirit, lovingly brooding always over our ships at sea and our camps at home and the battle line of our men at war, the spirit of a nation looking down in sympathy upon its sons.

They do not have that at home—our women. They only work and work and work for us, and then they pray. And pray for three things: First, that the war shall be soon over, and most earnestly may we join in that; and then that their men, whoever they may be, will come home again alive out of the struggle, and we can again join in that. But we cannot promise; that is on the knees of the gods, in the hands of fate. We may go home; we may not; we cannot control our destiny. And then they pray that, if we do come home, we shall come as clean and decent and upright and honourable gentlemen as we left—and we can do that. Nowhere in the world does a man stand more squarely on his own feet, to make or mar his character, than in the military service. We can go home clean if we want to. So remember always, if you want to go back worthy to look your women in the face, if you want to go back and have them glad you came and not sorry that some kindly bullet did not leave you on the field of honour over there—it is up to you, men; it is up to you.

CHAPTER XVII

SOME REFLECTIONS ON THE WAR

IT MIGHT be wiser, perhaps, if I were to leave all critical discussion of the war in general and the problems growing out of it to those trained writers and thinkers who have made a special study of these things. Viewing the situation broadly from afar, their ears unassailed by the roar of cannon and the groans of dying men, a clearer perspective is granted them. But they are for the most part civilians, and my only excuse for indulging in these closing reflections is that the views of a professional soldier, whose life has been spent with the Marines and who has faced the Boche on the firing line, may be not without a certain interest for those who gain most of their conceptions of the war from magazine writers and the editorial pages of the daily papers.

Before the war the German army was spoken of as the finest military organization the world had ever seen. Now that it has been defeated I have sometimes been asked what I think of it. Well, the military man still has the highest respect for the German military genius. We must give the devil his due. Strictly on military lines, it would have been absolutely impossible to beat the German military organization with anything like equal numbers.

That organization was so perfect in every department, that each man counted for more than any other single man in the world. And their capacity for speedy mobilization was unexampled.

In the second place, the German system of strategy, carefully and methodically developed by generations of military geniuses, was practically flawless, and the German general staff was at least the equal of any in the world. And in the present war the reputation of that staff and that system of strategy has been amply justified. In Foch the German strategists met their match, but their system is still unassailable; they never were beaten on strategy.

How, then, shall we account for the downfall 'of the all-powerful German Empire? I think their failure must be attributed to fundamental defects in the German psychology and the basic error of their belief that might can rule the world in spite of right. They have utterly misunderstood the moral motives and mental processes of other peoples; they were mistaken in their belief in the German type of discipline as affecting the fighting capacity of the individual soldier; they underestimated the duration of the war and hence overestimated their own resources and staying power.

While the German military strategy has been almost perfect, many of the German war measures have been fatally blundering. Their military judgment has amounted to an almost infallible instinct; their political judgment has often proved itself to be quite

unintelligent.   On numerous occasions their diplo-
macy has broken down completely.

The German theory of frightfulness is absolutely
logical if viewed only from a military point of view.
To destroy the morale back of an army is as effective as to destroy the morale of the army itself.   If
you are out to destroy, why not destroy both root
and branch?   What the German in his blind following of his faith in force failed to foresee was that in
neutral nations there existed a psychology which
would react against this theory of frightfulness and
so multiply Germany's opponents.   He was hoist
by his own petard.   If Germany had not murdered
babies in Belgium, if she had not ravished northern
France, if she had not destroyed cathedrals or
bombed hospitals or sunk the *Lusitania*, if she had
not, in short, followed out her theory to its logical
conclusion, the United States, loving peace, might
never have entered the war, and the Hun would
have been in Paris to-day.

The Germans, judging all men by their own char-
acteristics, misjudged the capacity of both the opposing commanders and the opposing troops.   Measuring them by a fixed, mathematical standard, they
wrongly estimated their power in the field.

And the Kaiser's own carefully prepared armies
failed him in the eleventh hour.   The German
calculators failed to figure in the correct percentage
of depreciation.   The Kaiser started the war with
a military establishment 100 per cent. efficient.   It
was a perfectly adjusted machine.   But the individ-

ual parts of it weakened; the machine ran more and more out of gear; and the Kaiser, knowing only how to use a perfect mechanism, resorted not so much to the strengthening of the weaknesses as to the general repairing of the machine. During the last year of the war he was running with a patched engine, and a patched engine is not the thing he knows how to run. In the four years of fighting the Germans lost heavily in officers and a large part of their best troops were used up. What they had left were not a match for the flower of American manhood pitted against them.

The German soldiers and the German people became war-weary. As far back as last spring we learned from prisoners that they were beginning to feel that they could not win the war. They had begun to distrust their leaders; rust was getting into the German machine.

In this policy of deceit, in the belief of the German ruling class that the common people could be made to believe anything indefinitely, there lay one of the greatest of German blunders. It had nothing to do with strategy, but it was a fundamental defect in their military theory.

In other words, the 100 per cent efficiency failed because of fatal errors of judgment. The German leaders misjudged Belgium, and France was given a few precious days in which to prepare for the first Battle of the Marne. They misjudged England and brought against them the power of the British navy, and later, the wonderful British armies. They misjudged the British colonies; they misjudged the United States. All the brilliance of their military genius and all the perfection of their system of strategy could not avail against such basic errors of judgment. Germany credited all men with selfish motives and an elastic code of honour, and, thank God, Germany was wrong.

One has also begun to wonder about the individual German soldier, that perfect creation of the German machine, who at last began to lose his nerve and cry "Kamerad." Unquestionably he was the best trained soldier in the world, and no military man underestimates training. Not even the French soldier was his equal in that respect, while we in America have little conception of how thoroughly every German was made over into a soldier. Individually he was no coward, particularly when supported by his fellows and his officers in a mass movement, as has been demonstrated on a hundred occasions. What he lacked was initiative, resourcefulness, adaptability, the very things the United States Marines have always sought to develop. Furthermore, the German soldier is, as a rule, a poor marksman, while the average American is a natural shot. I think I am safe in saying that there are no finer marksmen in the whole world than the United States Marines, and I doubt if our boys would ever have been able to take those machine guns in Belleau Wood if they had not picked off four or five Germans with their rifles for every American that fell. The German soldier, with all his training, can be licked by a

Frenchman or a Canadian, and I believe that to-day, man for man, the American troops are far superior to the over-rated Germans in personnel.

It is difficult to characterize the American soldier; it is hard not to brag. To the British and French veterans who have learned all there is to know about war during these four bloody years, we are still a bit raw. But they all concede that the American possesses courage, dash, initiative, a strong morale, and a splendid physique. Perhaps it would not hurt us to exhibit a little more modesty in the face of events, but one cannot suppress a thrill of pride when some battered old French Territorial glances up from his trench digging with a broad smile at the husky Yankee swinging by, waves his hand, and cries with Gallic generosity, "Bon soldat! Bon soldat!"

I believe that our part in this war has been vital, that if we had not gone in Germany would have won. The morale of the French people was unquestionably at low ebb; they had begun to lose hope. Our first troops got there none too soon, but even though they were a bit slow at getting into the fighting, their mere presence on French soil served to hold up Foch's hands and brought back hope to the French people. Our critics over here did not all believe that these things were so, but the French knew. The mere fact that half a million Americans were training on French soil was enough to hearten volatile France. They needed something more than mere fighters, and they got it in the nick of time.

And if the United States Marines had not beaten

back the Hun at Belleau Wood, Paris might easily have fallen, and what would have happened to French morale then?

For morale may win or lose a battle or a war, and the Americans, whatever else may be said of them, were bubbling over with confidence.

One matter has been settled by this war which my association with the Navy has led me to be particularly interested in. The U-boat campaign was a failure. It has been demonstrated that the submarine is not the most formidable naval weapon after all. The speed, efficiency, and resourcefulness of the Allied torpedo boats and destroyers have removed that question from the realm of debate.

Well, the war is over, and we all rejoice in that. There has been enough of killing and of suffering. But it has not been fought in vain if Germany's military power has been thoroughly broken and its menace to civilization ended forever. We must remain constantly on guard to prevent the development of any similar malevolent power elsewhere.

Never was there a conflict of human wills so fraught with peril and despair as this one, nor so pregnant with hope for the future of the human race. We are proud that we had a part in it. Nor need we, I think, reproach ourselves or our Government for not taking a fuller part. We did what we were given to do and God knows it was no child's play. We went in with clean hands and we came out with hands soiled only with the blood of international criminals.

So much for the conclusions to be drawn from the

military lessons of the war. In moral and ethical fields it has taught us much. Especially have our eyes been opened to new truths regarding preparedness, efficiency, discipline, and democracy.

We have heard a lot about preparedness since the *Lusitania* was sunk, but I am inclined to think that a good deal of it is but dimly understood. It seems to me that the first premise to be established is that the thing to be prepared for is likely to be of supreme and vital importance. It is one thing to keep your revolver loaded on general principles; it is quite another to be informed of the fact that burglars are operating in the neighbourhood. The Marine has learned that there are always burglars operating in some neighbourhood, and his revolver is always loaded. As for the Nation, I am not surprised that Americans were slow to wake up to the necessity for preparedness, for they did not believe in burglars. It took a lot to convince them. But perhaps the lesson has been learned and the Nation will never become quite so completely demobilized again. So long as human nature is what it is, so long as there is a bare possibility that burglars like the Potsdam gang may be in existence somewhere, it is best to be ready.

Discipline is a thing that the average American must more fully comprehend and believe in if he is to become a thoroughly effective and trustworthy citizen, if the principles of American democracy are to be justified. So far as it signifies serfdom, the free American is right to condemn it. But when it becomes part of a creed based upon truth, when it subordinates individualism only so far as to perfect coöperation, when it means simply organization and team-work, when it stimulates rather than dulls personal intelligence and initiative, when it takes into account that man lives not to himself alone but is essentially a social being, when, in short, it is the result of a broader vision, then discipline becomes necessary to all national progress and the forward march of human civilization. Such discipline is quite different from the Teuton idea of utter subserviency to the State. To such discipline the wise man submits while the fool rebels. He sees in it a means of achieving the common good, which includes his own. He is but conforming with universal law, to combat which is suicide.

It is this ideal of discipline, combined with courage, will, and ability to act, that the Marine has learned in the hard school of experience—an experience more vivid and more varied than commonly falls to the lot of man. A study of the ideals and creed of the Marines, as exemplified by the history of the Corps, is, I believe, a study of Americanism of a type that is needed to invigorate, vitalize, and stabilize our body politic and make us proof against those political maladies and weakening influences which, as history so clearly teaches us, insidiously beset the prosperous nation.

National discipline we need. We have not yet learned to obey the law as the soldier understands obedience. We are an undisciplined people. Team-work and coöperation are in their infancy with us. And yet it would be a sorry day for democracy and for us if we were to fall under the ban of Teutonic efficiency, with the individual entirely subordinated to the State, which, after all, was created by man for man's benefit. Let us set up no man-made idols to fall down before and worship. Let us beware of the subtle lure of over-organization that leads to bureaucracy, that deadly feeling of security in the benevolent power of the machine. I speak of these things because they are going to be questions that we shall need to be awake to now the war is over and we find ourselves struggling to extricate our limbs from the net that we have in the emergency woven.

No military man can afford to say a word against efficiency in its better sense, for efficiency is the chief asset of the military establishment, but I doubt whether we have so much to learn from the Germans on that score as we thought we had. I fancy the word will become less of a shibboleth with us than it was before the war. We have already come to look upon it with suspicion, like all other things made in Germany. The Teutonic principles of efficiency as applied to education, government, and industry are too mechanical to fit in with American ideals. They leave out of account the soul of man, and leaving the soul out of account is the basic error of the Teutonic theory of life.

As to democracy, two sorts have been brought to our attention, the personal and the broadly social. When two strong men stand elbow to elbow amid the naked realities of battle, caste appears as a futile and artificial thing, without significance. Merit is the only criterion. And I trust that our young men will come back to America with fresher and clearer ideals of equality and brotherhood.

I have heard some comment as to the relation of British and American officers to their men. I have heard it said that we have much to learn from the French in the matter of personal democracy. Well, there is no hobnobbing between our officers and men, no casting aside of class distinctions, no informal slappings on the back, and I am sure that that sort of thing is far less prevalent in the French army than has occasionally been reported by imaginative writers. That sort of thing is incompatible with discipline, and discipline is the soul of any military establishment. At the front the men must salute the same as in camp. They must obey promptly and must show proper respect for their superiors. None of the snappiness of Marine discipline is dropped, for that discipline is essential on the battle front if anywhere.

Still, I doubt if a more cordial feeling of comradeship exists anywhere in the world than between our Marine officers and their men. It is based on consistent justice and on the confidence of the men in the unselfish devotion of their officers to the service and to the personal welfare of their commands. And there at the front we seemed to draw closer together, like members of a big family with common aims and interests at heart. There is nothing approaching servility in the proud Marine, but a ready acknowledgement of authority through a complete understanding of its necessity. If you had seen our Marines fighting at Belleau Wood, you would have become convinced of their implicit confidence and trust in their officers. And that trust was not betrayed. Those American boys who have enlisted in the Marine Corps since the war broke out have learned something, I believe, of the fundamental relationship of man to man and have caught some inkling at least of the truth that respect for properly constituted authority and personal democracy are not incompatible.

I hope, when they come back, it will be with the deep-seated conviction that a man's money and his social and business prominence do not necessarily make him superior in political judgment or entitle him to power or privilege. The spirit of Bolshevism is abroad in the world to-day, and if we would avoid its excesses we must beware of a post-bellum reactionary movement tending toward special privilege, the strengthening of class distinctions, and the benefit of the few at the expense of the many. Let us shun all political theories based on the false doctrine of the divine right of the successful business man to rule. That, rather than old-world aristocracy, is our American danger.

And considering democracy in its broader sense, let us never lose sight of the ideals that have been crystallized in the heat of this war—the ideals of justice and fair dealing among all nations and groups of mankind.

I hope the war will have aroused us to the importance of these questions. What its effect will be upon those young Americans who left their peaceful pursuits to shoot Germans, it would be difficult to say. I suppose some of them will be ruined by it all, physically and morally. There are always soldiers who are spoiled for an industrious career in time of peace; there are always some whose upset nervous systems make them useless citizens forever after. Following the Civil War the great army of tramps sprang into being; there may be something like that, only now we know how to handle those things better and have already begun to tackle the problems of post-bellum rehabilitation and employment.

One thing I am sure of, and that is that our modern American military discipline is going to benefit every man who has entered the service. They are all young men, and the influence of this thing will not be fully felt for a generation perhaps. But they will come back with a better command of themselves, and I look for a sturdier, more virile race of citizens in the United States of America.

I must leave it for deeper students of such matters to discuss our national problems after the war— political, economic, social, industrial. They lie outside the province of the military man. There will be a scramble for trade. There will be political upheavals. Labour conditions will be woefully upset. Business will be off its feet. And all our old problems of before the war will be revived to an intensified degree. I can only beg my fellow countrymen to be on guard against these things and pray that statesmen may be raised up with sufficient wisdom and clearness of vision to solve these problems. When the excitement of war is over, let us not sink back into complacent inactivity. Like the Marines, let us be ready and awake.

And finally I pray for a more robust and heart-felt patriotism, a genuine love of country like that which the Frenchman feels. So many of us have gone our ways, getting and spending, with little thought of our obligation to the land that gave us birth and the government that holds secure our sacred liberties. Can we ever again feel like that, I wonder? Can we meet a man who left an arm or his eyesight in France and pass on without a thought of what it was all for? Can we ever again look upon Old Glory as a mere banquet-hall decoration? Can we read what our college boys did in Belleau Wood without thanking God that the soil trod by Washington and Lincoln, the Pilgrim Fathers and the builders of the great West, can still produce men of such stuff as that?

It is my country that went into this war solely to save the ideals of Christianity from destruction. It is my country that sent the flower of its manhood to fight and die for that cause. It is my country that stands here on the great Western continent, facing the future with faith undimmed, ideals untarnished, in the full strength of her prime, the world-acknowledged champion of the rights of man. God save my country!